UNBELIEVABLE FOOTBALL

First published in Great Britain in 2019 by Wren & Rook

ISBN: 978 1526 362552 1
E-book ISBN: 978 1526 36243 8

10 9 8 7 6 5 4 3 2 1

FSC

Wren & Rook
An imprint of
Hachette Children's Group
Part of Hodder & Stoughton
Carmelite House
50 Victoria Embankment
London EC4Y 0DZ

An Hachette UK Company
www.hachette.co.uk
www.hachettechildrens.co.uk

Publishing Director: Debbie Foy
Senior Editor: Laura Horsley
Art Director: Laura Hambleton
Designed by Claire Yeo

Printed in the United Kingdom

UNBELIEVABLE FOOTBALL

WRITTEN BY
MATT OLDFIELD

ILLUSTRATIONS BY
OLLIE MANN

wren & rook

CONTENTS

INTRODUCTION

Introduction

Some football fans think they know it all, don't they? From Roberto Firmino's favourite car to Northampton Town's 'next big thing' (that's Jay Williams, just in case you were wondering), they seem to have all the facts at their fingertips.

But if you really want to impress your footie-mad mates, then this is the book for you. Over the next 240 pages, you'll find out all about the most incredible true football stories you never knew. Such as the true tale of the greatest women's football team of all time, who played their last match in 1965. Or the player who faked his own death on the football pitch in 1977. And even an octopus who correctly predicted every result for Germany at the

2010 World Cup. Yes, an octopus!

You probably already have your favourite football stories, and we could play the 'Why didn't you choose ...?' game until the end of time but, if we did, there would be no book! So, ***Unbelievable Football*** is a collection of what I think are the best and most unbelievable stories out there.

And there are chapters to suit all fans. There's **'War and Peace'** for people who say football and politics don't mix, and **'Overcoming the Odds'** for those who think being a footballer is an easy life. But perhaps you want to read about clever creatures who love the game but have never kicked a ball? Well, **'Amazing Animals'** is for you. Or maybe you prefer football fairy tales about teams that never gave up? Try **'Unbelievable Comebacks'**. Then there are the cunning cases of mystery and mistaken identity in **'Who Are Ya?'**, and the lifesavers and gamechangers in **'For the Love of the Game'**. And for those who just love everything about football, the weirder and more wonderful the better ... there's the whole book to enjoy!

My hope is that these stories will make you smile, gasp, laugh, and then want to share them with all your football-mad friends. Because whatever the time, the team, the theme or the place, there are two things that all of the stories have in common (other than football, obviously!)

The first is that when you read them, they'll make you think:

'No way, it can't be true!'

And the second is that once you've remembered that **all of the stories are real**, you'll say to yourself:

'Wow, football really is unbelievable!'

Sound good?

Time for kick-off!

CHAPTER ONE

WAR AND PEACE

The Christmas Truce, 1914

Football is more than just a game, more than just a group of people kicking a circular object around a field. It has the power to bring people together, whether it's fans cheering on their favourite team or young footballers playing with their friends in the back garden. And there are plenty of great and unbelievable stories of football uniting even the fiercest of rivals, such as Brazil and Argentina, or Gary Neville and Jamie Carragher. But one story that has gone down in history is that of the **Christmas Truce**.

On a summer's day in August 1914, the First World War broke out and thousands of brave young British soldiers signed up to fight for their country against

Germany. Their families hoped that they would be home by Christmas, but it soon became clear that the war would last a lot longer than that.

Well, if those fathers and sons couldn't come home for Christmas, then Christmas would just have to come to them. That December, 2.5 million letters and 460,000 parcels were sent to British soldiers, who were fighting the Germans along the Western Front in Belgium and France. The parcels were filled with games, sweets, chocolate and knitted scarves to keep the troops warm during the winter. Would their loved ones get to open their gifts on Christmas Day, the British people back home wondered? Couldn't all the fierce fighting stop, at least for a few hours?

The soldiers and their families got their wish. On Christmas Eve, a German army officer walked across 'No Man's Land', the space between the two lines of trenches, to deliver a message to the British. It called for a truce, so that everyone could celebrate Christmas in peace. The British agreed and so both sides laid their weapons down wearily. They were all homesick and tired of fighting. All they wanted was the chance to bury their fallen soldiers and then enjoy a rest and some fun.

As the daylight faded into night, the Germans lit candles and began to sing Christmas carols including 'Stille Nacht'. Recognising the tune, the British troops sang back with their own words – 'Silent Night'! It was a beautiful reminder that even in the middle of a violent war, there could still be a moment of peace, where people came together as fellow human beings, rather than enemies.

That friendly feeling continued on Christmas Day morning. Some soldiers even strode boldly out into 'No Man's Land'. It was usually a very dangerous place to be because there were guns firing from both sides of the trenches. However, not on that special day. Instead, the British and German troops met in the middle to swap items, take photos with each other, and care for their wounded soldiers. For the first time in months, the ear-splitting sound of gunfire was replaced by conversation and laughter.

And ... football! Yes, without a shared language to speak, it is said that in some places along the Western Front, the men connected over their favourite sport. According to the stories, all of a sudden, a football appeared, and the soldiers started kicking it around together on the frozen ground. Soon, they threw their caps and coats down as goalposts and began to play a game. So, was it Britain vs Germany? It's unclear whether there were actual teams or just the total chaos of everyone vs everyone!

Although the two sides were at war, they were able to play a friendly football match together, without even having a referee. Lots of soldiers chasing after one ball in their big clumpy boots doesn't sound like a sporting classic, but the beautiful game had still brought them all together for one day of peace.

Sadly this peace didn't last. In most places along the Western Front, the battles started again on the next day. Some senior officers worried that truces would undermine the war and wanted to stop them happening in future too. So, there was to be no repeat of the Christmas Truce for the rest of the First World War, which didn't end until 1918. However, that only made the Christmas of 1914 all the more special. The legendary day when the fighting stopped, and a football match started.

The Elephants Who Played for Peace

There are some things in life that you really shouldn't mix: water and electricity, pale skin and bright sunshine, fingers and glue, feet and jellyfish. What about football and politics? Well, it's a risky combination, but sometimes they can work together to make the world a better place. Especially if your name is **Didier Drogba**.

Drogba was born in 1978 in Ivory Coast, on the west coast of Africa. During the early years of his life, the country was in crisis, with rising levels of poverty and crime. It wasn't a very promising place for a young child to grow up in, but fortunately Drogba's uncle, Michel Goba, was a professional footballer in France and he offered his nephew a way out.

At the age of five, little Didier left his homeland and went to live with Goba. Didier had to leave his parents behind because they couldn't afford to fly with him to France. He missed them very much, crying every day at first. However, he was determined to make them proud by following in his uncle's footsteps. Didier decided to become a football hero in Europe but also back home in Ivory Coast.

Drogba grew bigger and stronger and better at football until, eventually, his parents joined him in France. Now, aged 15, he was ready to really kick off his sporting career. But he didn't make it to the big time straight away. He had to be patient and believe that his chance would come. So Drogba started at a small club called Le Mans in the French Ligue 2. He was sure that if he played well enough, one of the big teams would want to buy him.

The next step was a spell at Guingamp, where he

showed that he could shine at a higher level. Then in 2003, Drogba finally got his dream move to Marseille, the team that he had supported since he was a boy. And in his first season, he scored 32 goals! He led them all the way to the final of the 2004 UEFA Cup (which is now called the Europa League) and even won France's Footballer of the Year award.

After that breakthrough season, Chelsea came calling for him. Over the next eight years, Drogba became a club legend there, winning 12 trophies, including three Premier League titles and the Champions League in 2012. Drogba was their match-winning hero that night in Munich. First, his powerful header saved them from defeat and then he scored the last spot-kick in the penalty shoot-out. Chelsea were the new Champions of Europe!

But throughout all those happy football times in France and England, Drogba never forgot about his homeland. Since 2002, Ivory Coast had been fighting a violent civil war – a war between different groups of people within the same country. Each time he returned home, it was horrible to see what was happening to his beloved country that had changed so much since his childhood. Drogba really wanted to help make things better, but what could he do? He wasn't a politician; he was a famous footballer.

In fact, there was plenty that Drogba could do. First of all, he used those skills that he had learned from his uncle. He scored goal after goal to lead the Ivory Coast national team, who are nicknamed 'The Elephants', to their first-ever World Cup. In order to qualify, they needed to beat Sudan and, after their 3–1 victory, the ecstatic players sank to their knees on the pitch. It was a dream come true – 'The Elephants' were on their way to the 2006 tournament in Germany! It was an incredible achievement and one that could hopefully help to unite their divided country.

During the post-match celebrations in the dressing room, Drogba decided to speak out. He had just used his football skills to shoot Ivory Coast to the World Cup; now, it was time to use his fame to try to bring peace to his homeland. All across the country, the Chelsea striker was a superstar, a symbol of pride and success. The people would listen to him while he used football as a tool to bring the whole country together.

The dancing stopped as Drogba took the microphone and looked down the lens of a video camera. All of his teammates were there by his side, supporting their inspirational leader.

'Men and women of the Ivory Coast, from the north, south, centre and west. We proved today that all Ivorians can coexist and play together.'

Then, The Elephants dropped to their knees again, this time to ask fighters on both sides of the conflict to lay down their weapons and work together towards peace. They pleaded with President Gbagbo to put an end to the civil war.

The video ended with the Ivory Coast players singing together, 'We want to have fun, so stop firing your guns!'

'I HAVE WON MANY TROPHIES IN MY TIME, BUT NOTHING WILL EVER TOP HELPING WIN THE BATTLE FOR PEACE IN MY COUNTRY.'

Drogba and his teammates got their wish; the fighting finally stopped.

At the 2006 World Cup, Ivory Coast only managed to win one match and were knocked out in the group stage. However, The Elephants and their captain Drogba had achieved something that went far beyond the world of football. They had helped to bring peace to their nation.

In 2007, an agreement was signed, and national elections took place in Ivory Coast.

So, job done? Not quite for Drogba. The Elephants were due to play Madagascar in an Africa Cup of Nations qualifier in his home city, Abidjan, but instead he asked President Gbagbo for one more favour: to move the match to Bouaké.

The city of Bouaké had been the scene of lots of fighting during the civil war. By playing the game there, The Elephants could once more bring the nation together, and help people to put aside their differences. Again, Drogba got his wish. Before kick-off, members of both sides of the conflict stood side by side to sing the national anthem. A new Ivory Coast was born, and football had played a key part.

The Lancashire Lasses Who Changed Football

Do you want to hear something really, really unfair? Well, between 1921 and 1971, women in England were not allowed to play football on any pitches owned by the Football Association (FA). Fifty years without a proper, decent match – can you imagine? That's as long as Paris Saint-Germain has been a football club!

But it was especially unfair because, during the First World War (1914–18), women's football had become one of the most popular forms of entertainment. With the men away fighting for their country, the women had stepped up to take their places, both working in the factories *and* playing on the football pitches. And could they kick it? Yes, they could.

In fact, some female footballers became international superstars and huge crowds would come out to support them. And there was one totally awesome team that ruled them all – **Dick, Kerr Ladies.**

Dick, Kerr & Co was a factory based in the northern city of Preston, founded by William Bruce Dick and John Kerr. All day long, the women worked hard making weapons and equipment for the war so, during their lunch break, they wanted to do something fun. And what better than have a kickaround in the yard outside?

Sometimes, the women at Dick, Kerr just played against each other but, at other times, they joined in with the men. By October 1917, there weren't many men left at the factory and their team was doing really badly in the local league. So badly that one of the women joked, 'Call yourselves a football team? We could do better than you lot!'

And with that, Dick, Kerr Ladies were up and running. After a 'friendly' match against the men where the women's team triumphed, they were on to their next adventure ...

A local hospital for wounded soldiers was looking to raise money, and they asked the women at the factory to help. 'What about a music concert?' they suggested. The Dick, Kerr Ladies, however, had a much better idea:

'What about a football match instead?'

The date was soon set for the special charity game – 25 December 1917. They would get to play football on Christmas Day, but that wasn't even the best bit. The top local football club, Preston North End, let them use their huge stadium, Deepdale. Wow, there would be thousands of people watching!

But who would they play *against*? The Dick, Kerr Ladies sent an invitation to one of the nearby factories,

Arundel Coulthard. Challenge accepted!

So far so good, but the next step for Dick, Kerr Ladies was picking their team for the charity match. That part was a lot more difficult because almost every woman at the factory wanted to play. In the end, the manager, Alfred Frankland, held trials to find the best 11 players. They included captain Alice Kell, tough-tackling defender Lily Jones and the '2 Florries' in attack – Rance and Redford. It was a brilliant line-up.

After dinner on Christmas Day 1917, the Dick, Kerr Ladies finally took to the field, wearing black and white stripes on their shirts and on their hats too. Hats? Yes, they wore thick bobble hats to cover up their hair! As they walked through the tunnel and out onto the pitch at Deepdale, the players must have been full of nervous excitement. They could hear the cheers of thousands of voices. About 10,000 voices, in fact; it was easily the biggest crowd of the year!

All eyes were on Dick, Kerr Ladies as they kicked off in their football debut. So, how would they cope under the pressure? Well, as it turned out, very well indeed. They thrashed Coulthards 4–0 and raised £600. Not a bad sum now but back then, £600 was equivalent to £50,000!

At first, some of the supporters found the idea of women playing football strange and even a little silly. Not for long, though. Once they saw the talent in the Dick, Kerr Ladies team, they had no choice but to really take them seriously.

'We want more!' the fans cheered as the game ended, and the players all agreed. The Christmas Day charity match was such a huge success that Dick, Kerr Ladies became an official football team.

That Coulthards crushing turned out to be the first of many famous victories, at Deepdale and other stadiums around the country. In no time at all, the Dick, Kerr Ladies were so well-known that people even asked them for autographs and photos.

As the war went on, the interest in women's football grew and grew. Not only were teams like Dick, Kerr Ladies helping to keep the people happy during hard years of war, but they were also making important money for charity.

'Play up, Dick Kerr's! Play up, Lancashire!'

In the past, sport hadn't been seen as a 'ladylike' thing to do, but not any more. Female footballers were making the most of their new freedom and fame. They were showing that anything men could do, they could too! In that way, it was a really important step in women's fight for equality.

As Dick, Kerr Ladies got bigger and bigger, they also got better and better. Frankland started to strengthen the squad by taking the best players from other nearby teams. One of those was a tall, skilful striker called Lily Parr, who played for St Helens Ladies. What a signing! She was only 14 years old at the time, but she went on to score nearly 1,000 goals in 30 years at the club. Lily also became the first female player in the English Football Hall of Fame and she now has a statue in the National Football

Museum in Manchester.

In 1918, the First World War finally ended and the soldiers began to return home. Soon, the men's English Football League was starting up again. Uh oh, what would happen to the women's game now? Well, in fact, 1920 was the biggest year yet for Dick, Kerr Ladies. When a French team arrived for a tour of England, who did they choose to play against? Dick, Kerr Ladies, of course, the best team in the country!

Twenty-five thousand excited fans filled the Deepdale stadium for the first-ever women's international match. And who won? Dick, Kerr Ladies, of course – 2–0. The team then travelled to France for a fun European football adventure of their own.

But that amazing day at Deepdale was nothing compared to Boxing Day 1920. Dick, Kerr Ladies took on Lily Parr's old club, St Helens Ladies, at Everton's Goodison

Park in front of ... 53,000 people! And there were thousands more waiting outside the stadium who couldn't get a ticket.

It was a new record crowd for a female football match, and a clear sign of just how important and successful the women's game had become. Dick, Kerr Ladies had proved that they were just as talented and popular as any men's team.

'WOMEN WANTED TO WORK, THEY WANTED TO VOTE AND THEY WANTED TO PLAY.'

– Gail J Newsham

In 1921, Dick, Kerr Ladies had played 67 games against teams from England, Wales, Ireland, Scotland, Italy *and* France. A total of 900,000 people had come to watch them win ALL 67 of those games.

Yet despite their amazing success, there were dark days ahead for the women's game. After the war had ended, munition factories began to close, men went back to work, and the country started to piece itself back together. Some individuals believed that female footballers were getting a bit too big for their boots.

'Who do they think they are,' they asked each other, 'stealing all the limelight from us men?'

Many people began to think that women should return to their traditional role of looking after their families at home, rather than playing football in front of huge crowds. Thankfully, views have changed a lot since then but, in 1921, the FA also decided that football was 'quite unsuitable for females'. And that wasn't all. They came up with a really unfair new rule: women's football matches were no longer allowed to take place at FA grounds.

For Dick, Kerr Ladies, it was the worst news ever. That meant no more massive crowds at Deepdale or

Goodison Park. What were they going to do? Could they continue? The team would battle on bravely for another 44 years in the new 'LFA' (Ladies Football Association), first as 'Dick, Kerr Ladies' and then as 'Preston Ladies'. But, sadly, their golden, glory days were over.

Still, those 'Lancashire lassies' had already put their names down in the history books, thanks to their remarkable achievements on the football field. Kell, Jones, Rance, Radford, Parr and many others played a really important part in changing the role and reputation of women in British society. One hundred years later and women's football is now bigger and better than ever. And where would our modern heroes like Steph Houghton and Nikita Parris be without those brave and talented women that played before them? Not starring on the football field, that's for sure. So, for one last time:

'Play up, Dick, Kerr's!'

The Superstar Manager Who Survived the War

Béla Guttmann was determined to be a world-class football manager and he wasn't going to let anything get in his way – not even the Second World War. This war was fought over six years and involved many countries around the world. Many millions fought in the war and life became very difficult for everyone, even those not directly involved in the fighting. But out of this tough and terrible time came stories of human bravery, brilliance and resilience. Béla Guttmann's is one of them and he would go on to become one of the greatest football managers of all time.

After Germany invaded Poland in 1939, France and Britain declared war on Adolf Hitler's Nazi Germany. The

Nazis saw Jewish people as their enemies and, during the war, they sent them to concentration or labour camps, where millions died. This is now known as the Holocaust. By 1944, the Nazis had invaded countries across Europe, including Hungary. The Nazis then rounded up all the Jews that they could find in the capital city, Budapest. But among those that escaped was Béla Guttmann, a Jewish man who would go on to shape modern football.

Guttmann had already enjoyed a successful football career, playing as a central defender for clubs in Hungary, Austria and even the USA, as well as for the Hungary national team. By the time the Second World War began, Guttmann was 40 years old. He was no longer playing football but, instead, he was aiming to become a successful manager. That wasn't easy to do during wartime. Most sporting competitions had been cancelled, but he still went to watch as many matches as he could.

One day in March 1944, Guttmann was in the stands watching two Hungarian teams, Újpest and Nagyvárad, play each other when he heard the awful news: 'The Germans have marched into Budapest!'

Guttmann had already been forced to flee his birthplace once before, in 1922, just because he was Jewish. He had returned home to Hungary some years later to start his coaching career, but would he now have to leave again? No. This time, he decided to stay, but he would have to be very careful. He was going to need a safe and secret hiding place.

For the next few months, Guttmann lived in the corner of an abandoned attic, hoping and praying for the war to end. But there were no signs of it stopping and he was eventually forced out of hiding, captured by the Germans and sent to a labour camp. There, he had to work all day long in terrible conditions, with hardly any food or rest.

By December, Guttmann couldn't stand the suffering and humiliation any longer. So, he and a small group of men he had met in the camp started planning their great escape. One day, as the camp guards swapped over, the gang made their move. They jumped out of a window onto some grass and then made a run for it!

Free again, Guttmann hid away until, in 1945, the Second World War finally ended. 'What now?' he thought to himself. It was time for him to return to his coaching career. After living through such terrible times, he wanted to make the most of his life and his love of football.

Guttmann wasn't going to let anything else get in the way of his special talent. He was a great leader, who knew how to get the best out of his players and help them win. After leading Újpest to the Hungarian league title in 1947, Guttmann set off on an amazing international adventure, managing clubs in Italy, Argentina, Cyprus, Brazil, Portugal, Uruguay, Switzerland and Greece. He never stayed long in one place – two seasons maybe, but rarely a third. Modern managers like José Mourinho seem to feel the same way!

Wherever he went, Guttmann stuck to his unique style of football. Although he had been a defender, he preferred passing to hoofing. He believed in all-out attack (unlike Mourinho!) and, during his time in Brazil, he even created his own 4–2–4 formation to achieve that. Yes, there were always plenty of goals when a Guttmann team was playing. In 1958, the Brazilian national team used his 4–2–4 formation to win the World Cup.

But Guttmann's greatest success came at Benfica, in

Portugal between 1959 and 1962. One day, as he was having his hair cut, he got chatting to a coach from Brazil. Their national team had just arrived in Portugal after a tour of Africa.

'Did you spot any talented players?' Guttmann asked.

'Yes, we played against this one outstanding young player in Mozambique,' the coach replied.

'Interesting!' After finding out as much information as he could, Guttmann signed the player for Benfica. It turned out to be the best deal he ever made. In his very first training session, the 19-year-old was simply unstoppable, dribbling past every defender. Guttmann smiled at his assistant and shouted, 'The boy is gold!'

'The boy' was Eusébio, who went on to become one of Portugal's greatest ever footballers.

With Eusébio on the field, Guttmann took his attacking style one step further. Instead of 4–2–4, Benfica often played a 3–2–4–1 formation. It all came down to a very simple idea:

'However many goals you score, we'll score more!'

It was a risky plan, but it turned out to be worth it because Guttmann's Benfica team went on to win back-to-back European Cups.

'I DON'T MIND IF OUR OPPONENTS SCORE THREE OR FOUR GOALS AS LONG AS MY TEAM SCORES FOUR OR FIVE.'

In 1961, they fought back from 1–0 down to beat Barcelona 3–2 and win the trophy for the very first time. Then a year later, they were involved in one of the best European finals ever. Hungarian superstar Ferenc Puskás scored twice to give Real Madrid a 2–0 lead, but Benfica came back brilliantly to win 5–3, thanks to two Eusébio goals and a cracker from Mário Coluna.

That amazing night in Amsterdam, Guttmann was at the peak of his coaching powers. Even now, nearly 60 years later, only three managers have won more European Cups than him: Liverpool's Bob Paisley, Carlo Ancelotti and Real Madrid's Zinedine Zidane.

Sadly, the 1962 European Cup turned out to be the last trophy that Guttmann ever won. He was a strong character and he was never afraid to speak his mind. He left Benfica that summer after they refused to give him a pay rise, saying, 'Not in a hundred years from now will Benfica ever be European Champions.'

At first, no one took those words very seriously but, since then, the club has reached eight European finals and lost every single one! In 1990, Eusébio even visited Guttmann's grave to ask him to end the curse.

Despite that, Benfica will always be grateful to their stubborn Hungarian boss. In 2014, they gave Guttmann his very own statue at the club stadium. It shows him dressed in a suit, holding his two huge European Cups, one in each arm.

The story of Béla Guttmann, however, is much bigger than just the trophies he won. After surviving the Second World War, he went on to become football's first superstar manager, mixing personality with tactical plans. Without him, we might not have the Mourinhos, Klopps and Guardiolas of today.

The War Adventures of the FA Cup Trophy

It was the spring of 1939 and plucky underdogs **Portsmouth** thrashed Wolverhampton Wanderers 4–1 in the final of the FA Cup, the oldest national football competition in the world. It was their first-ever triumph and a very proud day for the club as their captain Jimmy Guthrie collected the trophy from King George VI in front of nearly 100,000 fans at Wembley. But how long would the good times last? Well, it turns out 'Pompey' managed to keep the cup for seven long years, without even playing a match! And in those seven years the trophy would go on one epic journey around Portsmouth ...

That's because a few months after the final, the

British Prime Minister Neville Chamberlain declared war on Adolf Hitler's Germany, and the Second World War began. With so many young footballers going off to fight for their country, the FA decided to cancel all of their competitions. That meant no First Division, no Second Division, and no FA Cup! As the current cup holders, Portsmouth were asked to look after the famous, precious trophy.

'No problem!' said Jack Tinn.

Now, the Pompey manager was a pretty eccentric character. After his team lifted the FA Cup, he told everyone that it was because of his lucky 'spats' (they were like bibs that people wore over their shoes to protect them from splattering mud). Tinn had worn the same pair throughout the competition because he believed that had helped the team win. Before every match, the Pompey manager would get his right winger, Freddie

Worrall, to put them on for him. Maybe it was the smell that pushed Worrall forward to set up the fourth goal in the final!

Anyway, the Portsmouth boss now had a new job to do and he took his responsibility very seriously. For a little while, he even slept with the FA Cup under his bed at home. He wasn't going to let anything harm his beautiful trophy.

As the war went on, however, Tinn's task became more and more dangerous. The trophy was kept at the club's stadium, Fratton Park, but it soon became clear that Portsmouth really wasn't the safest place for it. The city was the home of the Royal Navy and that meant there was a high risk of bombing by the Germans.

The football club decided that the best way to protect the trophy was to keep moving it around the city. During those difficult years of war, the FA Cup became a source of great pride and joy for the people of Portsmouth. Together, they defended it heroically, just like their football team in the FA Cup final at Wembley.

One day during an air raid, Tinn was seen racing down the street with the FA Cup tucked under his arm. He had just rescued it from a shop window, but where was the best place for him to hide English football's most famous trophy? In the end, he found a pub and sat down in the cellar until it was safe to come out.

After that, Tinn decided to move the trophy to the deep vaults of a local bank. Surely, the FA Cup would be safe there? But no – one night, the German planes bombed the bank.

Oh dear, had the FA Cup been flattened like a pancake? No it hadn't, because Tinn had suddenly decided to take the trophy out of the vault that very morning. Somehow, he had known that something bad was about to happen to it!

Eventually, the trophy was taken out of Portsmouth and placed in a pub in a quiet Hampshire village. Like Tinn, the pub owner took his new responsibility very seriously. During the day, the FA Cup sat glistening behind the bar but, at night, it went upstairs and slept under the landlord's bed. And that's where the FA Cup stayed until the war was finally over.

Despite all of its perilous adventures, the trophy had survived the Second World War. And thanks to the people of Portsmouth, it was still in excellent condition. In fact, the only damage it did have wasn't because of bombs; it was because of one of the 'Pompey' players. Their FA Cup hero Bert Barlow, who scored in the final, had taken the trophy to an event and dropped it! He had paid for the repairs, though; his manager made sure of that.

When the FA Cup restarted in 1945, Portsmouth were desperate to win it again. The city loved that trophy and they didn't want to let it go. It felt like part of the family now. Sadly, however, their team lost 1–0 to Birmingham City in the Third Round. In April 1946, after looking after the trophy so lovingly for seven long years, Tinn had to hand it over to the new FA Cup winners, Derby County. It would be another 62 years before Portsmouth finally won it back again. But at least they still have their proud record as the holders of the FA Cup trophy for the longest period of time.

Aston Villa's Stolen Trophies

As you've just read, if you've got a trophy that needs protecting, give it to Portsmouth. If, on the other hand, you've got a cup that you don't really care about, let me recommend **Aston Villa**. Over the years, the club has lost not one, but TWO trophies.

The first was the FA Cup, way back in 1895. After beating local rivals West Bromwich in the final, the football club allowed shop owner William Shillcock to display the trophy proudly in the window of his store. They would soon regret that act of kindness ...

You can probably guess what happened next – one night, the trophy disappeared! A big reward was offered for any information, but the FA Cup was never found. In the end, Villa had to pay for a brand-new trophy to be made.

In 1958, an old man from Birmingham called Harry Burge claimed that he was the person who had stolen the FA Cup. And what had he done with the sparkling silver trophy? Melted it down to make fake coins, he told the newspaper! Whether that's true or not, we'll never know. Burge wasn't the most reliable of characters and he died in 1964.

But if losing one trophy is unfortunate, losing two is just plain careless. In 1982, Aston Villa beat Bayern Munich to win the European Cup. It was the club's greatest ever achievement and the celebrations went on for weeks. Even so, after the FA Cup mystery of 1895, you might have thought that Villa would keep a very close eye on such an important trophy. But no, instead they let two of their players, Colin Gibson and Gordon Cowans, take it to a local pub. What could possibly go wrong there?!

After a few drinks, they started playing darts. And in the heat of the game, the Villa players somehow totally forgot about the huge, valuable trophy they were supposed to be looking after, until someone shouted, 'The Cup's gone – it's been stolen!'

Luckily for Gibson, Cowans and everyone else at Aston Villa, this particular trophy wasn't lost for long. A few nights later, a man walked into a police station in Sheffield – about 100 miles away from the fateful pub – and delivered one of the best sentences ever:

'Excuse me, I've got the European Cup in my car.'

After the mysterious man had handed it over, the police officers had a great idea. Why not play their own European Cup final? It was a very competitive kickaround because the winning team would get to lift the actual trophy!

Since then, Villa have only added five more items to their trophy cabinet: a European Super Cup, two League Cups, an Intertoto Cup and, in 2019, the Championship play-off trophy. Let's hope the club is looking after them properly this time.

CHAPTER TWO

OVERCOMING THE ODDS

The Shepherd Boy Who Stopped Ronaldo

Anyone can kick a football around, but it takes real determination to make it to the top. Many of the best players and teams of all time have had to overcome huge odds to achieve their dreams. Whatever the obstacles in their way – age, gender, family, birthplace – their passion for football has pushed them forward.

One such person is **Alireza Beiranvand**. At the 2018 World Cup in Russia, Portugal were beating Iran 1–0 when their star man, Cristiano Ronaldo, was fouled in the box. *Penalty!* Pretty much everyone expected the five-time Ballon d'Or winner to score it, especially 'CR7' himself. He had scored his last six spot-kicks in a row, but not this one. The Iran goalkeeper sprang up off his line to make the save and then scrambled across the grass to grab the rebound. What a hero! It was a magical moment for that man, Alireza Beiranvand, and the highlight of a long and remarkable journey.

Alireza was born in Sarabias in south-west Iran but, for most of his childhood, his family moved all over the country, working as shepherds. That was Alireza's first job, but his first love was football. Whenever he could, he rushed off to join in with the local kickarounds. Like so many youngsters, he couldn't get enough of the game.

When Alireza turned 12, his father got a different job and so his family settled down in Sarabias. Alireza was delighted because that meant that he could start playing football for a proper team. At first, he dreamed of being a star striker but, one day, his team's goalkeeper got injured, so he stepped in. And guess what? Alireza turned out to be a great goalkeeper!

He was tall and athletic, but his superpower was his almighty throw. Alireza's right arm was as powerful as his right foot. He could launch the ball from one end of the pitch to the other to set up goals for his teammates. That was thanks to hours spent playing a childhood game called 'Dal Paran', where you have to throw stones as far as you can. Alireza must have been the local champion!

The more matches he played in goal, the more determined Alireza was to follow his football dream. He didn't want a normal job like his father wanted him to have; he wanted to save shots from superstar strikers in front of thousands of fans. It wasn't going to be easy, but he was going to become a professional player, no matter what.

So, one day, Alireza made a bold and very scary decision. He left his family behind in Sarabias and travelled to the capital city, Tehran, where all of Iran's top teams played. Can you imagine leaving home at such a young age? Poor Alireza had nowhere to stay and no club to play for, but, by a completely amazing piece of luck, he met a football coach on that long bus ride. Hossein Feiz listened to the boy's story and eventually invited him to come and train with his team.

But that was far from the end of Alireza's extraordinary story. He was still homeless in a new city, and he spent his first days in Tehran sleeping on the streets outside the football club. Thankfully, generous people passing by gave him enough coins so that he could buy food for breakfast.

Once he found a safe place to stay, Alireza worked harder than ever to achieve his aim. They say football is a game of two halves and so was Alireza's life. Half the time, he was a great goalkeeper, getting better and better, and half the time, he was doing any job he could find to make some extra money:

In a factory making dresses.

In a car wash scrubbing dirty vehicles.

In a pizza shop serving food.

And finally in the streets and parks of Tehran, picking up rubbish.

It was exhausting and disheartening work, but even then, when his professional football dream seemed so far away, Alireza still didn't give up. He would find a way, somehow ...

After many jobs and even more football teams, Alireza finally got his time to shine. From the Naft-e-Tehran Under-23s, he moved up to the club's first team and then to the Iran national Under-23 squad. The former shepherd boy was really going places now! His football dream was alive and kicking.

And throwing too. In 2014, Alireza's rocket launcher of a right arm became a YouTube sensation. In a match against Tractor Sazi, he caught a cross and then chucked the ball 70 yards downfield to set up Gholamreza Rezaei to score. The footage instantly went viral – it's one of the quickest counter-attacks you'll ever see.

Suddenly, the whole world was watching, including the Iran national coach, Carlos Queiroz. He called Alireza up for the national team and, in 2015, he made his international debut in the Asian Cup. That was a really proud moment but Alireza was soon thinking ahead to his next goal: helping his country to qualify for the 2018 World Cup in Russia.

Not only would that be an incredible achievement for Iran, but it would also be the perfect way for Alireza to show off his skills on football's biggest stage. Maybe he could even earn a dream move to the English Premier

League and follow in the gloveprints of his heroes like Manchester United's Edwin van der Sar ...

And why not? Alireza had already risen from street cleaner to star keeper! He believed that he could do absolutely anything if he worked hard enough.

First, however, he needed to become Iran's first-choice keeper. That wouldn't be easy because Alireza Haghighi was older and much more experienced. He had played at the 2014 World Cup and for top clubs in Russia and Portugal. But as Iran got ready for their game against Guam, Haghighi was told that he would have to stay at home because he didn't have the right travel visa.

At last, Alireza's big opportunity to start! With 70 minutes played, everything was going according to plan. Iran were 6–0 up and Alireza was minutes away from one of his favourite things in the world – a clean sheet. But then, disaster struck. Guam played a long ball over the top and Alireza rushed out of his penalty area to try to clear the danger. That was his intention, but he fouled the striker instead. *Free-kick! Red card!*

In his first-ever competitive match for his country, Alireza had been sent off. And to make matters worse, Iran had already made all three substitutions, so one of their defenders had to go in goal. It was a total disaster. This could have been the end of Alireza's World Cup dreams too. But luckily Queiroz believed in his great young goalkeeper. After serving his suspension, Alireza was straight back in the team. *Phew!*

With six wins out of eight, Iran cruised through to the third round of qualification, but things were about to get a whole lot harder. Now, they would have to beat much better teams, including China, Syria and Son Heung-min's South Korea.

Iran didn't score very many goals, but they

didn't concede many either, thanks to their great goalkeeper.

Iran 2–0 Qatar,

China 0–0 Iran,

Uzbekistan 0–1 Iran ...

Alireza was simply unbeatable! In ten games, only two shots got past him, and both of those goals came after Iran had already won their group. That's right, they were off to Russia to play at the 2018 World Cup ...

Alireza couldn't wait, especially once he knew who their opponents would be. Iran were in a tough group with two of the best teams in the world: World Cup 2010 Champions Spain and Euro 2016 Champions Portugal.

Only ten years earlier, Alireza had been sleeping alone on the streets of Tehran, hungry and scared. Now, he was preparing to go head-to-head with the world's best: Spain's keeper, David de Gea, and Portugal's striker, Cristiano Ronaldo. What a remarkable rise!

Alireza wasn't nervous, though; he was excited. This

was what he had been working towards since that brave trip to Tehran. All those long days and nights, all those other jobs, they had all been worth it because, now, he was playing at the WORLD CUP. His football dream had come true and he was going to enjoy every single second of it.

> **'I SUFFERED MANY DIFFICULTIES TO MAKE MY DREAM COME TRUE BUT I HAVE NO INTENTION OF FORGETTING THEM BECAUSE THEY MADE ME THE PERSON I AM NOW.'**

In the first game against Morocco, Alireza was Iran's man of the match and they won 1–0. It was a great start.

Next up: Spain. Alireza made a good save from Sergio Busquets, but he couldn't do anything to stop Diego Costa's winning goal.

'Well played,' said De Gea as the two keepers hugged

at the final whistle, but Alireza couldn't help feeling disappointed. Oh well, Iran still had at least one more World Cup game to go and, if they won, they could still go through ...

Alireza had already made a name for himself with his super saves and enormous throws, but could he do something truly spectacular in the final group game against Portugal? Just before half-time, Ricardo Quaresma gave Portugal the lead with an absolute worldie. Alireza stretched his long arm up but there was no way he could reach it. And then, minutes later, Cristiano won a penalty.

As he stepped up to take the spot-kick, Alireza knew that this was his time to shine. If Cristiano scored, Iran's 2018 World Cup was over. He couldn't let that happen. Alireza had studied the superstar's last few penalties and he had a clever plan to stop him.

Step 1: Stand totally still on the goal-line. Alireza wasn't going to give Cristiano any clues about which way he would dive.

Step 2: At the last second, dive the right way and make the save.

Step 3: Spring up quickly to grab the rebound before anyone else.

PENALTY SAVED – what a hero! Thanks to Alireza, Iran were still in the game and, in the last seconds, they equalised. That draw wasn't enough to send Iran through to the next round, but for their great, resilient goalkeeper, it was still an historic day. After all the ups and downs in his life, this was easily his greatest moment. Alireza would never forget the day he saved a penalty from one of the game's greatest-ever strikers. And neither would the footballing world.

Leicester City, the Unbelievable Season

Only six clubs have ever won the English Premier League: Manchester United, Blackburn Rovers, Arsenal, Chelsea, Manchester City and ... **Leicester City**! Yes, during the 2015–16 season, 'The Foxes' pulled off the pretty much impossible, beating all the top teams to the title. It just might be the greatest underdog story in the history of English football. But how did they beat all the odds and achieve the impossible?

Leicester City spent six happy seasons in the Premier League between 1996 and 2002 but, by 2008, the team had slipped all the way down to League One. It was a humiliating disaster for the club, but there was no time to wallow. If they didn't act fast, the Foxes might get stuck down in the lower leagues for years.

With the help of their new manager, Nigel Pearson, Leicester went straight back up to the Championship, but the road to the Premier League turned out to be longer and more painful. They lost in the play-offs in 2010 *and* 2013. But they didn't give up. In 2014, Leicester finally made it back to the big time, yet could they stay there this time?

'Yes, we can!' cheered the fans.

'Yes, we can!' cheered the players.

The team spirit was incredible. The Leicester City squad was packed with players who knew all about bouncing back from tough times:

- Goalkeeper Kasper Schmeichel had made the difficult decision to leave Manchester City after five frustrating loan spells
- Captain Wes Morgan had spent ten years at

Nottingham Forest, never quite making his Premier League dream come true

- Midfielder Danny Drinkwater had been sold by Manchester United, after spending 13 years at his boyhood club
- Winger Riyad Mahrez had worked his way up through the leagues in France, silencing the critics who said he was too small to play at the top level
- Striker Jamie Vardy had been playing non league football until Leicester signed him for a reported fee of only £1 million. That would turn out to be a total steal ...

With so many strong, resilient characters, the Foxes weren't going to go back down to the Championship without a real fight. From November 2014 until April 2015, Leicester stayed bottom of the Premier League, but their players never stopped believing. Just when they looked doomed, the team battled back to win seven out of their last nine games and climb out of the relegation zone. At the time, it seemed like an absolute miracle, but the loyal Leicester fans hadn't seen anything yet ...

It was a huge relief to be staying up, but what next for the club? It was time for some changes. Leicester waved goodbye to Pearson and replaced him with an experienced Italian manager called Claudio Ranieri. There were more new faces on the football pitch too. The club didn't have much money to spend but they spent it wisely. The best of all the bargains was N'Golo Kanté, a central midfielder who only cost a reported £5.6 million. That same summer, Manchester United paid over FOUR times that amount for the player Memphis Depay, who some United fans regarded as a massive flop.

Like his new Leicester teammate Mahrez, Kanté had started his career in France, where he was told that he was too small to be a top footballer. That hadn't stopped him, however, and after lots of hard work, he was about to become a Premier League star.

As the new season started, many football experts thought that Leicester would be relegated. The chances of them somehow winning the Premier League title? A massive 5,000–1!

But the Leicester players loved proving people wrong. They had that incredible team spirit, and now they also had a clear gameplan: defend together as a team and then score on the counter-attack.

The plan worked perfectly. At the back, Schmeichel and Morgan got better and better at stopping their opponents. After the team's first clean sheet of the season, Ranieri even bought them all pizza as a reward. It certainly helped that the Leicester backline had Kanté buzzing around in front of them. It was like the little

Frenchman was in 20 places at once!

Then, when the chance came, Leicester attacked. With the skill of Mahrez and the speed of Vardy, they were unstoppable. Soon, those two were the league's most lethal pairing. They scored 42 goals between them. Vardy even broke a Premier League record by finding the net in 11 games in a row.

At first, the Foxes fans were still just hoping to stay up but, before long, they had to change their expectations. Their team was doing way better than that. After losing only one of their first 17 games, Leicester were right at the top of the table!

'If Leicester win the Premier League,' their former player Gary Lineker, who presents *Match of the Day*, tweeted with excitement, 'I'll do the first MOTD of next season in just my undies.'

That only made the Fantastic Foxes even more

determined to reach their goal.

'No, there's no way they'll keep this up,' many football experts argued. 'Leicester's lucky run can't last forever!'

It wasn't about luck, though; it was about talent and teamwork. Those Leicester players were fighters and, together, they rose to every challenge they faced:

Chelsea at home? Mahrez set up Vardy and then scored a screamer of his own. *2–0!*

Tottenham away? In the 83rd minute, Robert Huth powered home the winning header. *1–0!*

Liverpool at home? Vardy scored two classic strikes on the counter-attack. *2–0!*

Manchester City away? Huth and Mahrez got the goals. *3–1!*

At last, the football world started believing in 'The Unbelievables'. Maybe Leicester could go on to lift the Premier League title after all. Why not? The team was playing with so much confidence and they were handling the pressure brilliantly. Even when they lost to Liverpool and Arsenal, they had the belief to keep bouncing back.

Nothing was going to stop them; not defeats, not draws, not even red cards. With 1–0 win after 1–0 win, Leicester edged closer and closer to their target. The excitement was building all across the city, but the players stayed as calm and composed as ever. The title race wasn't over yet ...

On 2 May 2016, the second-place team, Tottenham, travelled to Chelsea for a must-win match. If Spurs failed to pick up all three points, then Leicester City would be crowned as the new Premier League champions.

What a moment! Vardy invited all of his teammates to his house to watch the big game together. Would there be huge celebrations at the end? They hoped so.

At half-time, Tottenham were 2–0 up, but in the second-half, Chelsea fought back. *2–1, 2–2!*

At the final whistle, the Leicester players hugged and danced around Vardy's house. Against those odds of 5000–1, they had made their dream come true; they had won the Premier League title!

'THE FANS ARE DREAMING. KEEP DREAMING. WHY WAKE UP?'

– Claudio Ranieri

For the proper party, however, they had to wait another five days. The King Power Stadium was packed for Leicester's last home game of the season. There were over 30,000 fans inside and many hundreds more listening outside.

After a 3–1 win over Everton, it was finally trophy time. When Ranieri led his remarkable Leicester team out onto the field, they got a loud, heroes' welcome. It was such a proud achievement for the football club, and for the city too. The whole world was talking about the amazing Leicester story.

After all the players had collected their winners' medals, Ranieri and Morgan held the shining trophy together and lifted it high into the sky. Leicester City were the new Champions of England and they would be playing in the Champions League in 2016–17.

The Leicester City Premier League title dream had come true. And yes, Lineker did present the first *Match of the Day* of the season in just his underpants.

The Remarkable Rise of Queen Fara

Women's football has taken the world by storm and in recent years incredible players have emerged on the international stage. But it's not always been an easy journey.

In November 2001, the England women's team took on Portugal in a qualifying match for the 2003 World Cup. That night, a 17-year-old wonderkid made her international debut. That wonderkid was **Fara Williams**, an attacking midfielder who had just scored 30 goals in her first season for Chelsea Ladies. As she raced onto the pitch in Portugal, Williams looked calm and confident, a star in the making.

Behind the scenes, however, things were far from

perfect. What her England teammates didn't know at the time was that Williams was homeless. During her childhood, Williams had lived in south London with her mum and three brothers, playing football all day long in the caged pitch on their estate. Although she was a Chelsea fan and loved going to watch them at Stamford Bridge, winning at Wembley had always been her dream. For the boys that she played with, that didn't seem so crazy. They had seen so many of their heroes do it before – David Beckham, Steven Gerrard, Michael Owen ...

But for a girl growing up in the 1990s, it seemed almost impossible. The England women's team usually played in small stadiums around the country, and it was the same for the Women's FA Cup final. Wembley? No way!

Then one day, Williams' football dream suddenly felt even further away. When she was still only a teenager, she decided to leave home after a family argument. That first night, she wandered the streets of London, cold and alone. With nowhere else to go, Williams spent the next six years living on friends' sofas and in cheap hostels across the city. She carried everything she owned in a rucksack, which she slept beside at night.

At that stage, Hope Powell was one of the only people who knew about Williams' lonely, scary struggles. One day after a trip with the England Under-19s, the manager noticed that Fara was still hanging around. When Powell asked her where she was going, the young player could only shrug her shoulders sadly. 'I don't know,' she replied. So, Powell took her to a safe shelter and made sure that Williams had a warm sleeping bag.

From that day on, the England manager kept a close eye on her rising star. Powell encouraged Williams to believe in herself and start taking football seriously. Before, she had just played the game for fun but, with her talent, she could achieve anything she wanted. From the Under-19s, Williams rose quickly up to the England senior squad, keeping her homelessness a secret.

Even though her football career was going really well, Williams still wasn't making much money from it. These days, the Lionesses are all professionals, who are paid to play the game they love. Back in 2001, however, even world-class players like Williams couldn't survive on the small wages from women's football.

But during those tough times in her life, football was the one thing that kept Williams going. It was the one thing that gave her purpose and hope for the future, that got her out of bed early every morning. The sport was her passion, her special talent, and no one could take it away from her. Williams' setbacks off the pitch had only made her stronger and more determined on the pitch. If she kept persevering, hopefully one day, football would

help give her a home of her own.

Williams worked really hard to make that wish come true. She travelled the world with England, scoring goals at Euro 2005, World Cup 2007 and Euro 2009. In one game against Belarus, she even scored a hat-trick of stunning strikes! During that time, she also won the FA International Player of the Year – not once, but twice.

In 2004, just as she was becoming an international star,

Williams decided to leave London behind and move to Everton Ladies. There, she became known as 'Queen Fara', while winning the FA Women's Cup, the League Cup and the FA Players' Player of the Year award. She also found a second job she loved, working as a coach in the local community. That was thanks to the help of her club boss, Mo Marley. With so many supportive people around her, Williams settled into her new life and her new home. She no longer felt like she had to do it all on her own.

'THE DIFFERENCE FOOTBALL CAN MAKE TO PEOPLE IS INCREDIBLE.'

The future was starting to look a lot brighter, both for Fara and for the England women's team. The Lionesses made it to the quarter-finals of the 2011 World Cup, and then the semi-finals in 2015. The team was getting stronger and stronger, with Steph Houghton and Lucy Bronze at the back, and Fran Kirby and Toni Duggan in attack. And bossing the midfield, there was Jill Scott and 'Queen Fara'. It was Williams who scored the goal in extra-time to beat Germany and give England the bronze medal, their best-ever World Cup finish.

After all the pain and suffering during her younger years, Williams had really found her feet. Off the pitch, she was using her experiences to help coach women and girls at the Homeless FA and in England's Homeless World Cup team. And on the pitch, Williams signed for Liverpool and won two Women's Super League titles in a row. She had so many medals and trophies that she didn't know where to put them all!

There was only one thing missing now: that Wembley win she had been dreaming about ever since she was a kid.

Then in 2014, Williams heard some very significant

news. The FA Women's Cup final would be moving to ... yes, Wembley Stadium! She wouldn't get a better chance than this; she had to do whatever it took to reach that final. At last, Williams' dream came true. On 14 May 2016, her Arsenal team beat Chelsea in front of 33,000 fans. The young, football-mad girl had grown up to become a Wembley winner, after all.

Williams is now 35 and England's most-capped player, after making an amazing 170 appearances for her country. Sadly, she wasn't part of the Lionesses' squad for the 2019 World Cup, but manager Phil Neville has said that her international career is not necessarily over yet. And, as you now know, Williams is not someone who gives up on anything without a fight.

The Football Legend Loved by Everyone

It's time to talk about football's hottest topic: who is the greatest player of all time?

Modern fans will probably tell you it's Lionel Messi, or Marta, or Cristiano Ronaldo. More experienced fans, meanwhile, will shake their heads and argue for Diego Maradona, or Mia Hamm, or Pelé. But maybe we should ask Pelé, the 'King of Football' himself, for his opinion ... 'People argue between Pelé or Maradona. Di Stéfano is the best, much more complete.'

Whether you believe the Brazilian legend or not, **Alfredo Di Stéfano** is certainly the greatest player you've (probably) never heard of. That's partly because the Argentinian striker was at his best in the 1950s, before the days of colour TV. And it's partly because he never appeared at a World Cup, despite playing for THREE different countries.

So here's the fascinating life story of the footballer many people call 'The Legend'. Di Stéfano made his debut for the Argentinian club, River Plate, at the age of just 17. He soon became a superstar, winning two league titles and scoring 55 goals in 75 games.

And Di Stéfano wasn't even a traditional striker. He was so talented that he could play almost anywhere on the pitch – in defence, in midfield, on the wing or up front. He had it all: stamina, strength, speed *and* skills. As top players like Pelé, Eusébio and Bobby Charlton all said, Di Stéfano was the complete footballer.

After achieving everything he could in Argentina, Di Stéfano moved to Colombia, where he won lots more trophies at Millonarios. What next? He needed a new challenge, but where? These days, the top European clubs are always looking to sign the star players in South American football, but not in the early 1950s. Back then, it was too expensive and exhausting for their scouts to travel that far. And at that time, the Argentinian was already 27 years old.

Di Stéfano, however, found a way to get to Europe; he was far too good to ignore. When Millonarios travelled to Spain on a football tour, he quickly caught the attention of the country's two biggest clubs: Barcelona and Real Madrid. In the end, it was Real who won the battle to sign him and Di Stéfano became their first global superstar, or 'Galáctico', 50 years before the likes of Ronaldo, Luís Figo and Zinedine Zidane.

But how well would South America's finest footballer perform against European defences? At the time, Di Stéfano was one of the only foreigners in an otherwise

Spanish team. For that reason, the man they now called 'The Blond Arrow' had his doubters at first, but he proved them all wrong. Di Stéfano lifted the La Liga title in his very first season and was the top scorer with 27 goals. Real then went on to win it again in seven of the next ten seasons!

And they didn't just dominate Spanish football during those years; with their amazing Argentinian number 9, Real destroyed the whole of Europe.

In the first-ever European Cup final in 1956, Real were 2–0 down against French club Reims, when Di Stéfano made a late burst into the box to score and inspired an incredible comeback. They had won the cup!

In 1957, he opened the scoring against Fiorentina from the penalty spot. Yet another European Cup win and his sensational performances that season also earned him the first of two Ballon d'Or awards.

In 1958, Di Stéfano found the net again in a 3–2 win over Italian side AC Milan. That made a third European Cup win.

In 1959, his unstoppable shot helped Real win their fourth European Cup.

But could they make it five in a row? Yes! Di Stéfano saved his best performance of all for that 1960 European Cup final against Eintracht Frankfurt. Real thrashed the German club 7–3, with hat-tricks from Di Stéfano and his Hungarian strike partner, Ferenc Puskás.

Di Stéfano's first two goals were simple tap-ins, but the third was a thing of beauty. He dribbled forward from near the halfway line and shot powerfully past the keeper from the edge of the penalty area.

'Oh my goodness!' the TV commentator cried out.

That made it five finals, five victories and seven goals for Di Stéfano. After making that bold move from

Argentina to Spain, he was now the undisputed king of European club football.

But what about the international game? Sadly, that wasn't such a successful story, despite Di Stéfano's best attempts. It all started so well. He made his Argentina debut in the 1947 South American Championship. He scored six goals in six games and guess what? They won the trophy. He really was the footballer with the golden touch.

But when Argentina refused to play at the 1950 and 1954 World Cups, Di Stéfano decided to switch and play first for Colombia and then Spain. He was desperate to star on the international stage. Spain failed to qualify for the 1958 tournament, but four years later, they succeeded, thanks to Di Stéfano's goals and determination. This would surely be his last chance, at the age of 36. But just weeks before the tournament began, he picked up an injury and couldn't play.

It was a huge disappointment for Di Stéfano, and there was one more dramatic setback to come in his career. A year later, Real Madrid travelled to Venezuela on a pre-season tour. One day, Di Stéfano was relaxing in his hotel room when the phone rang.

The voice on the other end told him that the police were downstairs, waiting to speak to him. Really? Di Stéfano thought one of his teammates must be playing a prank and so he put the phone down. But a few minutes later, there was a knock at his bedroom door.

No, this was no prank. Men with machine guns barged in, grabbed Di Stéfano and then bundled him into the back of a car.

'This is a kidnap,' they told him as they stuck bandages over his eyes.

What was going on? Why him? Di Stéfano tried his

best to stay calm under pressure, like he did on the football pitch, but he was terrified. 'They're going to kill me,' he thought to himself.

Fortunately, these kidnappers weren't a violent gang or criminals wanting money; they were a local political group who were looking for more publicity. What better way to get the Venezuelan people's attention than by taking the most famous footballer in the world hostage?

For two days and nights, Di Stéfano had to stay in a locked room, playing chess and card games with his kidnappers. Then on the third day, once it had become big world news, they bundled him back into the car and dropped him off safely on a street corner near the Spanish embassy.

After surviving the scariest experience of their life, most 37-year-old footballers might think about stopping, but not Di Stéfano. He even played a football match a few days later, before flying home to his family! And he went on to score 17 goals during the 1963–4 season, leading Real Madrid to yet another Spanish League title and yet another European Cup final.

This time, 'The Legend' lost, but Di Stéfano will be remembered as a winner, a pioneer, a complete player, and perhaps the greatest footballer ever. Nothing could stop him, not even being kidnapped.

The Girl Who Just Wanted to Play

'Age is just a number.' People like to say that a lot. Or, 'You're only as old as you feel.'

And over the years, football has proved that heroes do indeed come in all shapes and ages. At one end of the range, you have Candelaria Cabrera. She's only eight years old, but she has already made a name for herself in the world of football.

'Cande' has loved the sport ever since she got her first football, aged four. Her dream is to become one of the best players in the world, just like her fellow Argentinian, Lionel Messi. They even come from the same region of Santa Fe. And on the football pitch, Cande already has plenty of that Messi magic. In 2016, she started playing for her local team, Huracán de Chabás. Although she wears the number 4 on the back of her white shirt and often plays in defence, she's got serious skills in attack. But playing football hasn't always been easy for Cande.

Cande is a very strong character, and she's had to be because she's the only female in her entire football league. At first, some of the boys and their parents laughed at her and made cruel comments, like 'You can't lose to a *girl*!' But nothing they said could stop Cande from playing her favourite sport.

In 2018, however, her football career was in danger. The rules in Santa Fe stated that once she turned eight, she would no longer be able to play with the boys at Huracán. Instead, she would have to find a girls' team to play for. But how? There weren't any where she lived.

When she heard the news, Cande was devastated. It didn't make any sense; she just wanted to play football!

It was her favourite thing to do, so why did it matter if she was a boy or a girl?

'What did I do wrong?' she cried tearfully to her mum, but Rosana had no answer to that.

It wasn't fair, so Cande decided to fight. Just like when she was out there on the pitch playing football, she would keep going, no matter what. She posted a video on Facebook, explaining her situation, and the response was incredible. Estefanía Banini, the Argentina captain, wrote to her, telling her not to give up, and so did lots of her country's other female footballers. They all had similar tales of frustration and discrimination, as they battled their way to the top. 'We're with Candelaria,' they said. National team legend Belén Potassa even came down to Huracán to meet Cande and give her some special coaching.

It was great to see the female footballers of Argentina coming together, but could it lead to change? Yes! Thanks to their support, Cande was allowed to carry on playing for Huracán until the end of the season. After that, the local league would hold a big meeting.

Cande waited anxiously for the results of that meeting. Would it be more bad news? No, it was the opposite. The league created its first-ever female department, and announced that, from now on, boys and girls were allowed to play together in the same team until the age of 11, rather than 8. Then, from the age of 12, clubs would be able to register all-girl teams.

It wasn't yet the football equality that Cande was hoping for, but it was still a leap in the right direction. By speaking out so bravely, she was helping to build a brighter future for young female footballers all over Argentina. She even got to star in an inspirational new Nike advert.

But most importantly, Cande can keep playing the sport she loves, dreaming of one day starring for her favourite football team, Boca Juniors. And hopefully her younger sister, Rufina, will join her there too.

The World Cup Star Who Saved His Best until Last

From Cande, a future superstar, let's go to the other end of the football age range, and to a former superstar who isn't as famous as he should be – **Mr Roger Milla**.

Milla is best known for his goals (and celebrations) at the 1990 and 1994 World Cups, but by then Cameroon's greatest ever player had already enjoyed a long and interesting career. In fact, his fascinating football journey had started all the way back in 1970.

That's when he joined his local club, Léopard Douala, as a speedy, skilful, 18-year-old striker. In his debut season, Milla took the Cameroon league by storm, scoring 25 goals in just 29 games. And he didn't stop there. The very next year, he helped his club to win the Première Division title.

In 1976, Milla became the first-ever Cameroonian to be crowned the African Footballer of the Year. These days, the winners of that prestigious award – Pierre-Emerick Aubameyang, Riyad Mahrez, Mohamed Salah – all play for teams in the top leagues.. At that time, however, Africa's finest footballers still mostly played back home in their national divisions.

But after seven years of scoring success, Milla was restless and ready for a new challenge. He felt like he had already conquered Cameroon. So, what next? It was time to test himself against the best teams in Europe.

Milla spent the next 12 years playing for clubs in France: Valenciennes, Monaco, Bastia, Saint-Étienne and finally Montpellier. He didn't score as many goals as he had back home in Cameroon, but he did win the French Cup twice! And by making that brave move,

Milla paved the way for future African stars like George Weah, Samuel Eto'o and Didier Drogba.

However, the story of Roger Milla isn't really about club football; it's about his incredible international achievements. Milla started playing for his country in 1973 and scored six goals to help Cameroon qualify for their first-ever World Cup in 1982. No African nation had ever got through to the knockout rounds of football's greatest tournament. Could 'The Indomitable Lions' break that record? The answer, sadly, was no (for now). Cameroon didn't lose any of their group games, but they didn't win any of them either. After three draws and only one goal, they headed home in disappointment.

That could so easily have been the end of Milla's World Cup career. He led Cameroon to victory in the Africa Cup of Nations in 1984 and 1988, but the team failed to qualify for Mexico '86. And by the time Italia '90 came around, Milla had retired from international football.

But when 'The Indomitable Lions' qualified for the tournament, the President of Cameroon Paul Biya made a very important phone call.

'Come back!' he pleaded. 'We need you!'

By then, Milla was already 38 years old, and ending his excellent career on an island in the Indian Ocean. Were his best footballing days behind him? Perhaps, but there was only one way to find out. He couldn't say no when his nation needed him.

In their first match in Italy, Cameroon pulled off one of the biggest upsets in World Cup history. They managed to beat Diego Maradona's Argentina 1–0. At the final whistle, the players celebrated like they had won the whole competition!

That day, Milla only came off the bench to play the last ten minutes. However, it was long enough for him to impress his coach, Valeri Nepomniachi. The veteran striker clearly still had the speed and skill to become a World Cup star. So, in Cameroon's second game against Romania, Milla came on with 30 minutes to go and the score at 0–0. The manager's message was simple: get a goal!

In the 76th minute, Cameroon hoofed a high ball downfield for Milla to chase. The Romanian defender decided to let it bounce, and that's when Milla pounced. He jumped up bravely and chested the ball down. He was in the penalty area now, with just the goalkeeper to beat ... GOAL!

Not only were Cameroon winning, but Milla had just become the World Cup's oldest ever goalscorer! He ran over to the corner flag and danced around it, wiggling his hips and waving his right arm.

Ten minutes later, Milla was doing his dance again. He got the ball on the edge of the penalty area, beat one defender and then fired an unstoppable shot into the top corner. After a quick shake of the hips, the 38-year-old was too tired to carry on, so he fell to his knees instead, with a huge grin on his face. As he knelt there, the Cameroon fans clapped and cheered for their inspirational comeback king.

All over the world, people were copying Milla's goal celebration. It was the dance craze of the summer. Cameroon's striker was the talk of the tournament, and he wasn't done yet.

For the first time in their history, Cameroon were through to the World Cup round of 16, where they faced Colombia. Again, Milla came on early in the second-half with the score at 0–0. On this occasion, however, he didn't find the net straight away and so the match went to extra-time.

Another 30 minutes of football – would 'old man' Milla last that long? Well, as we said earlier in this chapter, 'age is just a number'. He seemed to have the freshest legs on the field.

In the 106th minute, Milla skipped past one tackle and burst into the box. No keeper in the world could have saved his thunderstrike. GOAL!

Two minutes later, it was game over. Milla stole the ball off the Colombian keeper, René Higuita, and passed it into an empty net. GOAL!

Somehow, he even had enough energy to rush over to the corner flag and dance in front of the fans yet again.

With four goals, Milla was now one of the top scorers in the competition, and Cameroon were into the

World Cup quarter-finals. The Indomitable Lions had become the first African team to ever get that far. But unfortunately, that's where their remarkable journey ended. England beat them 3–2, thanks to two penalties from Gary Lineker.

'ON THE TEAM I BROUGHT THE SPIRIT OF COURAGE AND AS A TEAM WE WENT AS FAR AS WE COULD.'

That 1990 World Cup felt like a fitting way for Milla to end his international career. His goals earned him the African Footballer of the Year award again, 14 years after his first triumph. So, time to finally hang up those shooting boots?

No, Milla still wasn't ready to say goodbye. Four years later, he was back in the Cameroon squad for USA '94, at the amazing age of 42. Surely, he was past it now? Some thought that he might just be there to give advice to the youngsters, but the manager Henri Michel brought Milla on against Brazil and then let him play the whole second-half against Russia.

By then, Cameroon were already 3–0 down and heading home. But at least Milla got to have his last dance.

Less than a minute after coming on, the ball bounced to him on the edge of the penalty area. A Russia defender rushed in to make a tackle, but Milla was so strong that he shrugged him off. Stretching out his right leg, he guided the ball into the bottom corner. GOAL!

'The old man has not lost the magic!' one TV commentator declared.

Cameroon's legendary striker had broken his own record. Milla had scored a goal at football's biggest tournament at the age of 42 years and 39 days. As he ran over to the corner flag, there was a wave of the right arm but, understandably, a little less wiggle in his hips.

That wasn't even the end of Milla's football career: he played club football in Indonesia for another two years, scoring on average more than a goal a game before finally hanging up his boots in 1996. Now he will be remembered as many things:

- a World Cup hero and history-maker
- one of Africa's greatest-ever players
- a dancefloor icon
- a man who always made football look fun, and
- an inspiring reminder that you're only as old as you feel.

Beach Ball Scores the Winner!

As you've just read, the magic of football is that anything can happen. The greats of the game come in all shapes and ages, and from all over the world. And that's just the players. Even objects can be gamechangers ... Over the years, many weird items have found their way onto a football pitch: false teeth, a cabbage, a flip-flop, even a pig's head. There's only one heroic object, however, that has scored a winning goal ...

In October 2009, Liverpool travelled to Sunderland in the Premier League. Their fans decided to bring along some toys for the long journey, including a big red beach ball with the club badge on it. Once they were inside the Stadium of Light, the Liverpool supporters blew it up and played a bit of volleyball. It was all fun and games until someone took it too far. They batted the beach ball so hard that it landed on the pitch!

And it didn't just drop down near the corner flag; no, it landed right in the middle of the Liverpool penalty area. Their goalkeeper Pepe Reina tried to kick it away, but the beach ball wasn't going anywhere. It was determined to join in the action.

In the fifth minute, Sunderland pushed forward on the attack. Lee Cattermole passed to Andy Reid, whose cross eventually reached striker Darren Bent at the back post. His shot wasn't the best, but it got a big helping hand from ... yes, that's right, the beach ball!

The real ball bounced off it and changed direction completely. Reina was a very confused keeper indeed – which ball was he supposed to save? In the end, he didn't save either. The beach ball went wide of the post, but the real ball flew past him, and into the back of the net. GOAL!

Some of the Liverpool defenders threw their arms up in protest, while others pointed at the naughty beach ball. They were all shouting the same thing, though:

'NO GOAL!'

The Sunderland players, however, were already celebrating. So, all eyes were on the referee – what would his final decision be? Unsurprisingly, he'd never seen anything like it. He didn't know what to do. According to the rules of football, he should have disallowed it, but instead, Mike Jones gave the goal.

Sunderland 1 Liverpool 0. Scorer: Beach Ball (Bent claimed the goal, though).

Ninety-two minutes later, that turned out to be the winning goal, and Sunderland moved above Liverpool in the Premier League table. Boy did those fans regret bringing that beach ball along!

'These things happen,' said the Liverpool manager, Rafa Benítez. But no other beach ball has scored a goal in the ten years since that match, nor in the 140 years of football before (as far as we know).

CHAPTER THREE

AMAZING ANIMALS

Pickles the Dog Detective

It all began at the start of 1966 and England was preparing to host the World Cup for the very first time. There was lots of excitement about the tournament, but nervousness too. People would be visiting from all over the world, so it was important that the country put on a really good show, both on and off the football pitch.

On Sunday 20 March, the Jules Rimet World Cup trophy was on display at a grand exhibition in London. It was all part of England's plan to build up interest in the upcoming tournament. Lots of people went along to catch a glimpse of the golden cup, glistening in its display case. There were supposed to be security guards watching the trophy at all times, just to make sure that it was safe. However, that day, the guards decided to take a little lunch break. When they returned to the room, they found that the lock was broken, the emergency exit door was open, and the display case was empty! With less than four months left until the start of the World Cup, the trophy was missing!

The police got to work straight away. But after a week of searching for clues and speaking to suspects, they still didn't know where the World Cup was. It was so humiliating for the government and, to make it worse, FIFA were furious. How had England managed to make such a mess of their beloved tournament already? Other football nations, meanwhile, were outraged. 'I'm damned angry,' said Mr Erik von Frenckell, former president of the Finnish Football Association. How could England be trusted to organise a World Cup when they couldn't even look after the trophy?

If someone didn't find it soon, there was a danger that it might be too late. The trophy might have been melted down already and sold to make lots of money, and what then? Maybe they would have to cancel the whole World Cup!

All around the country, people were looking for the trophy. In the end, however, it was a dog who came to the rescue – a four-year-old black-and-white collie called **Pickles**.

Pickles was out walking one night with his owner, David Corbett, in south London, when he noticed a strange parcel wrapped in newspaper and string, lying by the wheel of a neighbour's car.

'Come on, Pickles!' his owner called out from a distance. 'Let's go!'

But the dog detective didn't budge. He knew that he had found something significant. Pickles kept sniffing and pawing the parcel until eventually, Corbett came over to see what was going on. As he stooped down to clip the lead around his dog's collar, he spotted the parcel that Pickles had sniffed out.

It looked very suspicious indeed. Should he touch it? What if it was a bomb? Corbett ummed and ahhed but eventually he picked the parcel up. It felt very heavy in his hand, so he decided to see what was inside. As he tore off the first bit of newspaper, he could see a metal plaque, with four words written on it: 'Brazil', 'West Germany' and 'Uruguay'.

With his curiosity growing, Corbett ripped off another bit at the other end of the package. What he found was a golden figure of a winged woman holding up a cup. In an instant, he recognised it. The pictures had been all over the newspapers and the TV too. Pickles the Dog Detective had discovered the World Cup trophy!

With his heart pounding with excitement, Corbett went straight to the local police station to show them the parcel.

'I think I've found the World Cup,' he said, placing it down on the desk.

Don't worry, he didn't take full credit for it, though. 'Pickles saw it first!' he explained. At first, the officers didn't believe that it was the famous trophy, but it did turn out to be the real thing.

Phew – what a massive relief! The World Cup trophy was found. A dog had saved England from a major embarrassment. Soon, Pickles was a national celebrity – everyone wanted to meet the hero who had saved the World Cup. For the next few months, he lived like a king, with champagne, caviar and big juicy bones in his dog bowl every day. Pickles was given a silver medal by the Dogs Trust, a free year's supply of dog food, and the 'Dog of the Year' award too. He travelled the country, opening Coventry Zoo, appearing on *Blue Peter*, and even starring in a movie. Corbett, meanwhile, was given a reward so big that he was able to buy a new house for himself and his dog detective.

No one was ever jailed for stealing the trophy, but never mind; the story had a much happier ending. At the 1966 World Cup, England made it all the way to the final, where they beat West Germany 4–2. For the first time ever, they were the Champions of the World!

Afterwards, their captain Bobby Moore climbed the

steps at Wembley to collect the Jules Rimet Trophy from Queen Elizabeth II. But if it wasn't for Pickles, there would have been no trophy, and maybe even no World Cup at all.

So to say a big thank you for all his help, Pickles was invited to be a guest of honour at the team's celebration banquet. It was the best night of his life. He had hugs and photos with all of England's heroes, including Moore, Bobby Charlton and manager Alf Ramsey. Then to top it all off, he was allowed to lick Corbett's plate clean!

Sadly, Pickles died a year later in 1967, but football fans around the world will always remember him as the dog that saved the World Cup.

Hennes the Goat

Lots of football teams have big furry mascots cheering them on, from an alligator called 'Fritzle' (VfB Stuttgart) to a zebra called 'Jay' (Juventus). None of those, however, can compete with German club 1. FC Köln. Their mascot is a real, live animal – **Hennes the Goat**.

Yes, you've got that right. A goat.

The Köln (Cologne) football team formed in 1948 and, to celebrate their second birthday, a local circus owner gave them the best gift ever: a goat! He was only meant to bring them a bit of good luck, but the team coach, Hennes Weisweiler, loved the goat so much that he made him the official club mascot and the animal was named after him.

Hennes the Goat quickly became a local celebrity, living in luxury at the Cologne zoo. Soon, his friendly face was everywhere: at the matches, in the newspapers, and even on the football club's badge.

But what about being a good luck charm? Well, Hennes helped Köln to win the league title in 1963, 1964 *and* 1978, as well as four German Cups.

By the 1990s, most mascots were just humans wearing animal costumes, but not in Cologne. For their fans, it had to be the real thing, not a cuddly fake. Hennes I passed away in 1966 and he was replaced with another goat mascot. Ever since, whenever a chosen goat retires or dies, the football club holds a big vote to select the next mascot. We're currently in the reign of Hennes VIII. He has his own TV adverts and a Facebook page too!

Now, this might all sound like a bit of fun but, trust

me, Köln take their beloved goat very seriously, as the club's striker Anthony Ujah found out in 2015. When he scored an important goal against Eintracht Frankfurt, he was so excited that he ran over and yanked Hennes by the horns.

Uh oh, Ujah was in big trouble. Stroking their golden goat was OK, but grabbing him aggressively? No one could get away with treating him like that, not even a Köln hero. In the end, he had to visit the zoo and say sorry to Hennes face to face.

'I was just so happy,' the striker tried to explain to the media, 'but I know that it was a mistake. I won't do it again.'

Despite his apology, Ujah left Köln at the end of that season. The message is clear; if you go up against Hennes the Goat, you will always lose.

The Dog that Saved Manchester United

Manchester United is now known as one of the richest and most successful super-clubs. But it hasn't always been that way. Back in 1901, the team was actually called Newton Heath and it needed to raise a lot of money and very quickly.

With time running out, the club decided to host a huge fundraising event at St James's Hall in Manchester. There would be lots of live music and exciting exhibitions, plus the captain Harry Stafford had a clever plan of his own. Knowing that a dog is a man's best friend, he brought along his big St Bernard, **Major**, and attached a collecting tin to his collar. The idea was that as the supporters stroked the dog, they would slip some money in the box.

Sadly, the whole day turned out to be a total disaster. Not only did Newton Heath not raise the money they needed, but Major went missing!

Stafford was wild with worry. Where could he be? Who would want to steal his big beloved pet? The Newton Heath captain looked everywhere for his dog and even offered a reward but, at first, there was no sign of him.

Eventually, Major was found by a pub landlord, who put a notice in the local newspaper saying that he had found a big St Bernard belonging to a Mr Harry Stafford. How did he know the name of the owner? Because there was a clever poem written on the dog's collar:

My name is Major,
Of Railway Street, Crewe,
I'm Harry Stafford's dog,
Who's dog are you?

However, by the time that Stafford answered the advert, Major had a new admirer.

John Henry Davies was a very wealthy business owner. He ran lots of pubs around Manchester, including the one where Major had been found. On one of his business trips, he saw the beautiful St Bernard and decided straight away that the dog would make the perfect birthday present for his young daughter, Elsie.

So, where would Major end up? At first, when the two men met to discuss the dog, they couldn't agree on what to do. Davies was desperate to buy Major, but Stafford most definitely didn't want to sell him. Later on, however, the Newton Heath captain got talking about his football team and their serious financial problems. The future really didn't look good for the club, especially after the fundraising disaster. Unless a rich hero came along soon, they might not be able to carry on ...

As he listened, Davies, a brilliant negotiator, sensed there was a bargain to be made, one that would suit both sides. He offered to save the football club and invest lots of money to improve it, just as long as Elsie could keep Major.

'Deal,' Stafford said at last, with a very heavy heart. No one should have to choose between their dog and their favourite football team. But he knew Major would be happy with Elsie and the club would be saved.

Now that he had a new home, Major couldn't be the club mascot any more. So, he was replaced by a goat called Billy – yes, football teams seem to love goats! Billy belonged to one of Stafford's teammates, Charlie Roberts. But sadly Billy died during their FA Cup celebrations in 1909. So maybe Major had a lucky escape, after all ...

Anyway, back to football. A few months after the

deal was done, Davies stood up in front of the fans and made two bold decisions as the club's new owner:

1) He changed the shirt colours from green and yellow to red and white.

2) He changed the name from Newton Heath to Manchester United.

The rest, of course, is history, but many forget the important role played by a missing dog called Major. If he hadn't got lost and made his way to that particular pub, Manchester United Football Club might not even exist!

The Police Dog that Rescued a Team from Relegation

The year was 1987 and English club Torquay United were less than ten minutes away from being relegated out of the Football League. On a sunny May afternoon at Plainmoor, they were losing 2–1 to Crewe Alexandra, and the fans were fearing the worst. Defeat could even spell the end for Torquay United Football Club, and then what would the locals do on a Saturday afternoon? It was now or never for 'The Gulls' but, out on the pitch, their nervous players were running out of hope *and* ideas. So if not them, then who else could save the day?

Step forward, **Bryn the Police Dog**. His job was to watch out for any trouble in the crowd, but suddenly he spotted a different kind of danger coming from the opposite direction. The Torquay right-back Jim McNichol was chasing the ball at top speed, straight towards Bryn and his master, Inspector John Harris, on the touchline. The German shepherd was trained to protect, so in a flash, he spun around and sank his teeth into the player's thigh. *Owwww* – talk about some fierce attacking play!

Weren't the police supposed to protect people, rather than hurt them? Bryn's bite had torn a hole in McNichol's shorts and an even bigger one in his leg. As he lay there on the grass in shock and agony, it seemed like a total disaster for Torquay. Not only were they losing the match, but now they were about to lose one of their star performers too.

'Stupid dog!' the angry fans shouted down at Bryn and Harris below. 'Oi, Police Officer, can't you keep him under control?'

But actually, the dog bite turned out to be an excellent

delay tactic for Torquay. While their poor teammate was down receiving treatment, the other players were able to get together and work out a plan. As they swigged from their water bottles, they got their breath back, and their belief as well.

'We can still do this!' their manager Stuart Morgan urged them on. 'Lincoln City are losing at Swansea, so all we need is *one* goal!'

It didn't look good for McNichol, but he refused to give up. In those days, teams could only make one substitution and Torquay had already made theirs. So if McNichol went off on a stretcher, they would be down to ten men. No, he couldn't let his team down, not when they really needed him. With a big bandage wrapped around his leg, the right-back got back up and carried on playing.

'McNichol, you're a hero!' the Torquay supporters clapped and cheered.

Suddenly, hope was spreading around the Plainmoor stadium again. The 90 minutes were up, but the referee added an extra 4 minutes of injury time. Game on!

Come on, you Gulls!

With their new-found energy, Torquay pushed Crewe Alexandra further and further back towards their own goal, until eventually one of their midfielders panicked. He gave the ball away to Gulls striker, Paul Dobson, inside the penalty area, and 'Dobbo' turned and fired a first-time shot into the bottom corner. GOAL – 2–2!

At the final whistle, the tearful Torquay supporters raced onto the pitch to celebrate with their players. It was a miracle – they were staying up! Dobson's last-minute goal meant that their rivals Lincoln City went down instead. This time, there were lots of happy hugs, and no more animal bites.

Poor McNichol had to miss most of the party because

he was busy getting 17 painful stitches to sew up his horrible leg wound. Still, if it wasn't for Bryn's brutal tackle and the injury time he caused, Torquay would probably have lost that match and lost their place in the Football League. Even McNichol could see that. So despite everything, he still went down to the local police station to shake paws with his attacker, who, in his own way, had saved the day for Torquay.

'A DOG SAVES TORQUAY – IT'S NOT A BAD HEADLINE, IS IT?'

– Stuart Morgan, manager

From villain to hero, Bryn became the talk of the town and the whole football world. The club chairman gave him two special gifts to say thank you: a big, juicy bone and a yellow and blue Torquay scarf.

Paul the Octopus

'What a clever animal!' People say that all the time. You hear it whenever their dogs/cats/lizards learn to sit/roll/bake cakes (OK, maybe not that last one), but if you want to hear about a properly clever creature, let me introduce you to **Paul the Octopus.**

Paul was born in a Sea Life Centre in the pretty British seaside town of Weymouth in 2008, but as a hatchling (that's what they call a baby octopus, by the way) he moved abroad to another Sea Life Centre in Oberhausen, Germany. It was there that people started to notice Paul's special talents.

The first sign that he was a really clever octopus was his ability to open jars and boxes as easily as a human being. That was a cool trick, but what else could Paul do, they wondered? Predict football results, perhaps?

The Sea Life Centre workers came up with a game to test him during Euro 2008. Before each match that the Germany national team played at the tournament, they placed two clear plastic boxes in front of Paul. Each box had food inside – either a mussel or an oyster – and a national flag on the front. Apparently, whichever box Paul opened first was the team that he thought would win the match!

'What about draws?' you ask. Well, sorry, that wasn't an option. But never mind, no one likes draws anyway ...

Paul's record at Euro 2008 was pretty good – four correct predictions out of six. Not bad for an animal that had never played – or watched – football in his life. Sadly, however, he messed up on the most important result of all. After getting Germany's hopes up by gobbling the food from their box, they ended up losing 1–0 to Spain in the final.

'Schlechte Krake!' (That's 'Bad Octopus!' in German ...)

Despite getting that one wrong, Paul got to keep his job for the 2010 World Cup in South Africa. By then, he was the most famous psychic octopus ever (probably). Thousands of football fans came to visit him in his tank and his predictions for the tournament were even shown live on German TV!

And this time, with the pressure on, Paul put on his best performance. He got every single result right – eight out of eight, one for each of his psychic tentacles. They included Germany's surprise defeat to Serbia in the group stage, their exit in the semi-finals and, best of all, Spain's victory over the Netherlands in the World Cup final. If you watch the online video for that prediction, Paul goes straight to the Spain box, without a single doubt in his mind. Now that really is a seriously clever animal.

By then, the Spanish people loved Paul like one of their own. When the football team returned home to a hero's welcome in Madrid, there were octopus banners everywhere and their captain Andrés Iniesta even held up a small soft-toy version of Paul.

With each correct prediction, Paul became more and more famous around the world. Forget Lionel Messi or Cristiano Ronaldo; the real star of the 2010 World Cup was in a tank, not out on the football pitch! An aquarium in Spain invited him to visit, while an angry chef from Argentina threatened to cook him after his country lost to Germany in the quarter-finals. Fortunately, the keepers at the Sea Life Centre protected their celebrity carefully. Paul stopped predicting football results after the tournament in 2010, and at his retirement party, they presented him with a mini World Cup trophy of his own (filled with tasty mussels, of course!)

'THERE ARE ALWAYS PEOPLE WHO WANT TO EAT OUR OCTOPUS, BUT HE IS NOT SHY AND WE ARE HERE TO PROTECT HIM.'

– Oliver Walenciak (Paul's keeper)

Sadly, an octopus doesn't live very long, even one as clever as Paul, and he died in October 2010, at the young age of two-and-a-half. It was a sad end for such a successful psychic, but at least, as the Sea Life Centre's manager, Stefan Porwoll, said, Paul 'had a good life'.

And the genius of Paul lives on. He has a giant monument at the Sea Life Centre in Oberhausen, as well as an iPhone app called 'Ask the Octopus' and even his own song.

Like all great heroes, Paul has also helped to inspire others. So far, we've had a sea turtle predict results from Brazil, a hedgehog from Thailand, an otter from Japan, a camel from Dubai, and even another octopus, this time from Ukraine. But none of them has come close to the legend that is Paul the Octopus.

CHAPTER FOUR

UNBELIEVABLE COMEBACKS

The Busby Babes

Sometimes when things go wrong on the football pitch, you might feel like giving up. But don't, because that's when the best teams show their true fighting spirit. Whether you're losing 3–0 at half-time or 31–0 at full-time, the incredible comeback is always on. Football fairy tales really do happen, and Manchester United is one of the greatest ever told.

Now, you may think the glory days of Manchester United were in the 1990s when players like David Beckham, Paul Scholes, Nicky Butt, Gary and Phil Neville, and Ryan Giggs dominated the game. Their manager, Alex Ferguson, had invested in them when they were playing in the club's youth team. And it had worked! They won the first-ever Premier League title in 1993, and the 'Class of '92', as they were known, went on to dominate English football for the next 20 years. But 'Fergie's Fledglings' weren't the first amazing young Manchester United team. No, that was '**The Busby Babes**' ...

Like Ferguson, Matt Busby was a Scottish manager who believed in giving youth a chance. He arrived at Old Trafford in 1945, just after the end of the Second World War. Four times in five years, his Manchester United team finished second in the First Division, once missing out on the title by one single point! It was very frustrating to keep getting so close to glory, but Busby, his assistant manager Jimmy Murphy and his chief scout Joe Armstrong had a plan. They were going to build an unbeatable team of the best young players around.

In the 1955–6 season, 'The Busby Babes' won the league by a whopping 11 points, with a team half filled with 'kids'. They included:

- Wilf McGuinness, 18, an energetic player who loved to get up and down the pitch
- Eddie 'Snakehips' Colman, 19, a skilful wing-back who could weave his way past anyone
- Duncan 'The Tank' Edwards, 19, a big, strong midfielder with a fantastic football brain
- David Pegg, 20, a tricky left winger with an eye for the goal
- Liam 'Billy' Whelan, 20, an Irish forward who could fire them in from anywhere
- Mark 'The Gentle Giant' Jones, 22, a tough-tackling defender
- Bill 'Foulkesy' Foulkes, 23, another rock at the back.

These youngsters played with class and confidence, entertaining crowds all over the country. Two years and another league title later, Manchester United moved on to their next target: European Cup glory. Now that they were the kings of English football, they were ready to take on the rest of the world. By then, 'The Busby Babes' also had a couple of very fresh new faces:

- Kenny Morgans, 18, a Welsh right winger with lots of speed and skill
- Bobby Charlton, 19, a midfield maestro with a ferocious shot.

But a terrible tragedy would change everything. On 6 February 1958, Manchester United were happily flying home after beating Red Star Belgrade and booking a spot in the European Cup semi-finals. This was going to be their year; the squad was sure of it.

But when the plane stopped in Munich, Germany, to refuel, it had trouble taking off again. There seemed to be a problem with the left engine, plus snow was falling thick and fast on the runway. The pilots decided to give it one more go and asked everyone in the airport passenger lounge to get back on the flight. Minutes later, that mistake would end in catastrophe. As the plane surged forward, it skidded on the snowy slush and crashed through a fence at high speed.

Tragically, 23 of the 44 people onboard died in what became known as the 'Munich Air Disaster'. Among those who lost their lives were supporters, journalists, three Manchester United coaches and eight players, including Colman, Edwards, Pegg, Whelan and Jones.

The whole football world was in shock. 'The Busby Babes', England's most exciting young team, had been torn apart.

What next for Manchester United? Could the survivors carry on? Despite suffering a head injury, Foulkes had managed to free himself from the safety belt and escape to safety. Morgans and Charlton soon recovered from their fairly minor injuries, while McGuinness had missed the trip because of a broken leg.

And what about their boss, Busby? Well, the Manchester United manager spent many weeks in hospital with very serious injuries. At first, the doctors didn't think he would survive, but he made a great recovery in the end. It was only then that Busby's friends and family told him the full truth about the tragedy. He was absolutely devastated to have lost so many of his young 'babes'. At first, he thought about quitting football and giving up on his Manchester United masterplan.

Thankfully, however, Busby didn't do that. Instead, he returned to Old Trafford and began rebuilding his Manchester United team. The painful memories of Munich would live on and push them forward. It was an ambitious project that would take years to complete, but eventually it would end in triumph.

The Reds bounced back, just like their manager had after the Munich Air Disaster and lifted the league title again in 1965, thanks to Foulkes, Charlton, and the brilliant new Busby Babes:

- George 'The Belfast Boy' Best, 19, one of the best dribblers of the ball the world had ever seen
- David Sadler, 19, a skilful centre-back
- Norbert 'Nobby' Stiles, 23, a ferocious midfield terrier who wore false teeth!

It was a new team, but they played the same old, exciting style of football. Three years and another league title later, the new Manchester United moved on to their next target: European Cup glory. The team was determined to win the trophy this time; for the fans, but also for the team of 1958. Ten years after the tragedy in Munich, victory would be theirs at last.

On 29 May 1968, Manchester United took on Benfica

in the European Cup final. What a moment it would be if the Busby Babes could win it in front of a huge home crowd at Wembley!

Charlton scored first early in the second-half with a clever flick header into the bottom corner, but with ten minutes to go, Benfica equalised. Noooooo! When the goal went in, the Manchester United players were distraught. They just stood there for a moment, with their heads in their hands. Was that it; was their European dream over?

No, because thanks to Busby's inspirational team-talk, Manchester United bounced back brilliantly in extra-time, scoring three goals in seven minutes.

Best raced through and dribbled around the Benfica keeper. *2–1!*

The latest Busby Babe, Brian Kidd, headed home. *3–1!*

Charlton curled a shot into the top corner. *4–1!*

'THEY CAME BACK WITH ALL THEIR HEARTS TO SHOW EVERYONE WHAT MANCHESTER UNITED ARE MADE OF ... I AM THE PROUDEST MAN IN ENGLAND TONIGHT.'

– Matt Busby

It was game over and, at last, Busby had achieved his target. Manchester United were the new Champions of Europe, and the first English club ever to win the cup. As the players celebrated on the Wembley pitch, it marked the end of one of the greatest comebacks in football history. Just ten years after his talented young side had been torn apart by the Munich Air Disaster, the Manchester United manager had built a new team of Busby Babes and taken them all the way to the top of European football.

The Miracle of Istanbul

There are many stories of teams who look set to lose miserably but then turn everything around at the last minute. On 7 May 2019, **Liverpool** pulled off one of the most incredible comebacks in football history. After losing 3–0 to Lionel Messi's Barcelona in their Champions League semi-final first leg, they somehow came back to win the second leg 4–0. 'That's our best win ever!' some Liverpool supporters said. But long before 'The Miracle of Anfield', their team was involved in an even better comeback: 'The Miracle of Istanbul' ...

Back in 2005, there was no Mohamed Salah, no Virgil van Dijk, and no Jürgen Klopp. Rafa Benítez was the Liverpool manager and Steven Gerrard was the club's inspirational captain. They also had Jamie Carragher in defence and Xabi Alonso in midfield but, other than that, there were no real superstars.

What that Liverpool team lacked in skill, however, they made up for in spirit. They didn't give up, no matter what, and they beat European giants Juventus and Chelsea to make it all the way to their first Champions League final in 20 years.

Could Liverpool now go on and win the trophy for the fifth time? It wasn't going to be easy because their final opponents were AC Milan. They had an amazing team, with world-class superstars in every position: Cafu and Paolo Maldini in defence; Andrea Pirlo, Clarence Seedorf and Kaká in midfield; and Andriy Shevchenko and Hernán Crespo in attack.

Did Liverpool stand a chance? Not in the first-half, where AC Milan absolutely thrashed them.

Maldini volleyed home Andrea Pirlo's free-kick. *1–0!*

Shevchenko crossed to Crespo. *2–0!*

Kaká played the perfect pass to send Crespo through. *3–0!*

As they trudged off the field at half-time, the Liverpool players looked shocked and distraught. They were 3–0 down – was it game over already? There didn't seem to be any way back for the Reds.

Their fans, however, weren't giving up yet. In fact, they sang so loudly and so proudly in the stands that the players could hear them clearly, even deep in the dressing room.

'We owe those supporters something special,' Benítez told his team as they sat there in silence, listening. 'We have to fight – we've got nothing to lose!'

The Liverpool players returned to the pitch with their belief back. They could do this! All they needed was one goal, and they would be right back in the game. That's why the manager brought on Didi Hamann in midfield and pushed his star man Gerrard further forward.

They say 'football is a game of two halves' and this match certainly was. As soon as the second-half kicked off, Liverpool came to life. In the 54th minute, John Arne Riise curled a cross into the box and there was Gerrard to score with a powerful, leaping header. *3–1!*

'Come on!' the Liverpool captain cheered. As he ran back for the restart, he waved his arms up and down, urging his teammates to keep fighting, and the supporters to keep making noise.

Suddenly, there was hope again. Liverpool had that first goal they wanted; now, they just needed two more. Alonso passed to Hamann, who passed to Vladimír Šmicer. The Czech midfielder was still a long way out, but he decided to go for goal. Why not? At the last second, his shot dipped and squirmed under Dida's arms and into the bottom corner. *3–2!*

Two goals in two minutes – their incredible comeback was on! The fans had brought the amazing Anfield roar all the way to Istanbul. Liverpool couldn't ... could they? They all dared to dream. With the crowd behind them, the players felt like they could achieve anything.

Three minutes later, Carragher dribbled forward and fed the ball through to Milan Baroš, who flicked it back to Gerrard. As the Liverpool captain pulled his left leg back to shoot, Gennaro Gattuso tripped him. *Penalty!*

This was it: the chance for Liverpool to complete a remarkable comeback. It was Alonso who stepped up to take the spot-kick. Although Dida dived down low to make the stop, the Spaniard slid in quickly to score the rebound. *3–3!*

The fans, the players, the managers – no one could

believe what had just happened. Six minutes earlier, Liverpool had been losing 3–0, and now the match was tied. It was turning out to be the most exciting Champions League final ever.

But how would it end? For the next 30 minutes, AC Milan's attackers tried to score the winning goal, but Liverpool's heroic defenders kept denying them. It stayed 3–3, thanks to Carragher's terrific tackles and Jerzy Dudek's super saves. Throughout those tense moments, their supporters never stopped singing:

Liverpool! Liverpool!

Eventually, after extra-time, the final whistle blew, and the 2005 Champions League final went all the way to penalties. Could Liverpool win the shoot-out and pull off probably the greatest comeback in football history? Their players hardly had any energy left, but they had more than enough passion to carry them through.

As Milan's Serginho placed the ball down on the spot, the Liverpool keeper Dudek danced across his goal-line, waving his arms above his head. He was trying to put the penalty-taker off, and it worked. The Brazilian blazed his shot high over the crossbar. What a start for Liverpool! Despite playing with a broken toe, Didi Hamann stepped up and ... scored. *1–0!*

Everyone thought that Pirlo was sure to score for AC Milan, but first the Italian had to get past Dudek, who was on fire. The keeper made a super save and then Djibril Cissé sent Dida the wrong way. *2–0!*

It was all looking so good for Liverpool, but then Jon Dahl Tomasson and Kaká both scored, while Riise missed. *2–2!* The supporters buried their heads in their hands. Was there going to be another twist in the tale? Hadn't they had enough drama for one night? Fortunately, Šmicer kept his cool to give Liverpool the lead again.

Right, this was it; the crucial spot-kick. Shevchenko had to score, otherwise it was all over for AC Milan. He looked calm and focused as he ran up, but he was about to make a big mistake. He tried to chip it over the diving keeper, but Dudek reached up his right glove and saved it. It was over: Liverpool were the new Champions of Europe!

'THE ENGLISH CLUB PROVED THAT MIRACLES REALLY DO EXIST. I'VE NOW MADE LIVERPOOL MY ENGLISH TEAM.'

– Diego Maradona

Dudek jumped high into the air as his teammates raced over to celebrate with him. The Liverpool players were all buzzing with excitement, but it was a while before their amazing achievement really sank in. From 3–0 down, they had battled back to win the 2005 Champions League final, against the best team in the world.

As Gerrard lifted Europe's top trophy, the club's players and supporters roared together, and red and white confetti filled the air. It was a particularly special night for Liverpool, but 'The Miracle of Istanbul' was a match that no football fan, watching anywhere in the world, would ever forget.

The World's Worst Team Who Didn't Give Up

If you think you're having a bad day, try losing an international football match 31–0. That's what happened to poor **American Samoa** in April 2001 when they travelled to Australia for a World Cup qualifier.

It was never going to be a fair fight; only 55,000 people live on the small Pacific island, compared to nearly 25 million in Australia. The American Samoa national football team didn't have any professional players and, before that nightmare match, they had lost every single one of their competitive games, putting them joint bottom of the FIFA world rankings.

Surprisingly, it took Australia ten whole minutes to score their first goal but, after that, the American

Samoa defence collapsed completely. Although their keeper Nicky Salapu made some excellent saves, he still spent most of his time picking the ball out of his own net, while looking increasingly frustrated. By half-time, it was 16–0 to Australia.

Now, you might think that was enough goals already, but 'The Socceroos' weren't satisfied. Two days earlier, they had thrashed Tonga 22–0 and, now, they had their sights on another new world record. One Australian player even took a shot straight from the kick-off!

At full-time, the scoreboard in the stadium read 'AUSTRALIA 32 AMERICAN SAMOA 0'. Actually, it was only 31, but the officials had, understandably, lost count in the second–half. Either way, American Samoa were the humiliated new holders of the record defeat in the history of international football.

'WHAT A JOKE,' read one newspaper headline.

'THE WORLD'S WORST TEAM,' read another.

What do you do after a defeat like that, when the whole football world is making fun of you? Some teams might have given up, but not American Samoa. Instead, the players stayed out on the pitch to sing a song for their supporters. After the match, their manager, Tunoa Lui, made a bold claim: 'In five years, we will be competitive.' To achieve that aim, they would need to take things one step at a time.

Step 1: concede fewer goals. That was nice and simple. In their next match against Tonga, American Samoa only lost by five goals to zero. They were making progress already!

Step 2: win a match. This one, however, took a lot longer to complete – ten years, in fact.

On 22 November 2011, American Samoa took on Tonga again in the qualifiers for the 2014 World Cup.

By then, pretty much everything had changed, except their goalkeeper Nicky Salapu.

That year, a Dutch manager called Thomas Rongen had accepted the job as American Samoa national team coach. It was only when he arrived on the island and watched a training session, however, that he realised the task that lay ahead. Turning American Samoa into a winning team was going to be the greatest challenge of his career.

Rongen set to work straight away, pushing his players hard to improve as individuals and as a team. The manager also called up players from the national youth teams and from US colleges as well. They spent hours practising their passing, sprinting, slide tackling and shooting. After a few tiring weeks of training hard together, it was finally time to test themselves.

American Samoa were determined to prove that they

weren't that same 'world's worst team' any more. As they walked out onto the pitch, led by their captain Liatama Amisone, Jr, they were fearless football warriors, ready to fight for the pride of their country.

Every player battled hard for the ball, but it was American Samoa's striker Ramin Ott who looked the most likely to score. He blazed his first shot over the bar and then struck the post from a free-kick. The number 9 was getting closer and closer ...

But in a flash, Tonga were on the counter-attack. As the cross came in, their striker was totally unmarked in the middle. Surely, he would score? But no, Salapu the American Samoa keeper saved the day with a brilliant block.

With half-time approaching, the score was still 0–0. Suddenly, Jaiyah Saelua passed the ball through to Ott, who was just inside the Tonga half. He spun quickly and went for goal again. It should have been a pretty simple save for the keeper, but the ball took an awkward bounce and slipped through his gloves.

AMERICAN SAMOA 1 TONGA 0!

What a special moment for the small Pacific island! The crowd went wild as Ott ran to the touchline with his arms in the air and his teammates piled on top of him. Could American Samoa now hold on for a historic victory?

They did much better than that. Rongen's side dominated the game with some flowing attacking football. American Samoa had come a long way since the dark days of 2001.

In the 74th minute, Shalom Luani raced onto a through ball. The Tonga keeper rushed out to tackle him, but Luani lobbed the ball brilliantly over his head and into the empty net.

AMERICAN SAMOA 2 TONGA 0!

Sadly, there weren't so many celebrations this time because Luani had been injured scoring his wondergoal.

'Keep going, the game's not over yet!' Rongen shouted from the sidelines.

The American Samoa players were running out of energy, but Salapu was there to rescue them again and again. The painful memories of that 31–0 defeat were still fresh in his mind. Only a win would make things better.

Tonga did pull one goal back with five minutes to go, but American Samoa held on for that historic victory.

AMERICAN SAMOA 2 TONGA 1!

Seeing the scenes at the final whistle, you might have thought that they had just won the World Cup. Some players sank to their knees on the pitch, while others raced around waving their arms in the air. It was the greatest and most emotional day of all their lives. After 17 years and 30 games of failure and frustration, American Samoa had finally won their first-ever competitive football match.

'It's like a miracle!' said Salapu with tears in his eyes.

'This is going to be part of football history, like the 31–0 against Australia was part of history,' said Rongen.

The manager was right; American Samoa were world news again and, this time, for the right reasons.

'FOR AMERICAN SAMOA, VICTORY AT LAST,' read one newspaper headline.

'AMERICAN SAMOA'S DREAM TEAM,' read another.

In the end, they didn't qualify for the 2014 World Cup, but who cares about that? Not their players, that's for sure. American Samoa had achieved their aims: to win an international match and bounce back from that dreadful day ten years earlier.

Amazing Zambia, Champions of Africa

The 'Chipolopolo' – the Copper Bullets – of **Zambia** were a fearless new generation of talented footballers and 1993 was going to be the biggest year for them yet. They were ready to take on Africa and then the world.

Zambia's success had started five years earlier, at the 1988 Olympics. After an exciting 2–2 draw with Iraq, everyone expected the Copper Bullets to lose to Italy. The Italian senior team had won the World Cup three times. How could poor little Zambia compete with their quality and international experience?

But at half-time, the underdogs found themselves winning 1–0, thanks to a goal from their striker Kalusha Bwalya. Could Zambia hold on for a famous victory?

Well, they did better than that.

Kalusha curled a clever free-kick into the Italy net. *2–0!*

Johnson Bwalya dribbled forward from midfield and scored a swerving 35-yard screamer. *3–0!*

Kalusha nutmegged the Italian keeper to complete his hat-trick. *4–0!*

Zambia 4, Italy 0. It wasn't just a win; it was a thrashing. Move over Nigeria, Algeria and Cameroon – Africa had an awesome new national team!

After that impressive performance, there were high hopes for the Copper Bullets. Zambia finished third at the 1990 Africa Cup of Nations and then lost in extra-time in the quarter-finals in 1992. That was a cruel blow, but their players were still full of confidence and ambition. They planned to become Champions of Africa in 1994 but, before that, they were going to qualify for their first-ever World Cup.

But disaster was about to strike. On 27 April 1993, the Zambia national team were travelling to Senegal for their next qualifier. A win would take them a step closer to the tournament in the USA. After a short stop for fuel in Congo, the plane took off again towards their destination. But minutes later the engines tragically caught fire and the plane lost power. The crash was a rare and tragic accident, and sadly no one survived.

Zambia couldn't believe the tragic news. How had such an awful thing happened to their beloved football team? Over 100,000 people lined the streets to remember the players outside the Independence Stadium in the capital city Lusaka, at a special monument called 'Heroes' Acre'. The nation would never forget their greatest-ever football generation.

But what now for the Copper Bullets? Two of Zambia's

key players weren't on that plane that day. Kalusha Bwalya was taking a later flight after playing for his Dutch club PSV Eindhoven, while Johnson Bwalya was recovering from an injury. They were so distraught at what had happened that they thought about giving up. It would be so hard to imagine playing in a Zambia national team without their teammates. The Senegal match had, of course, been delayed, but what about the World Cup and the 1994 Africa Cup of Nations?

The Bwalyas agreed eventually that they had to carry on playing in memory of their teammates.

In August, Zambia set off to face Senegal with an almost totally new young team and a new manager too – the former Chelsea boss Ian Porterfield. Unfortunately, the match finished 0–0 and the Copper Bullets missed out on their World Cup dream.

But, the Zambia story doesn't end there. In March

1994, their squad travelled to Tunisia to take part in the Africa Cup of Nations, just as they had always planned it. Kalusha and Johnson Bwalya were determined to make their missing teammates proud and bring joy to their mourning country. It wouldn't be easy with a new-look squad, but the team spirit was stronger than ever. The Copper Bullets had unfinished business.

After a 0–0 draw with Sierra Leone, Zambia took on Ivory Coast, the team that had beaten them in extra-time two years earlier. This time, they took their revenge. Sub striker Kenneth Malitoli scored the winning goal that sent Zambia through to another quarter-final. There, they faced their old rivals Senegal and beat them 1–0.

Zambia were on a roll, but were their players nervous about being in the semi-finals again? Not one bit. Poor Mali didn't stand a chance against their passion and skill.

Defender Elijah Litana headed home. *1–0!*

Zeddy Saileti tapped into an empty net. *2–0!*

Captain Kalusha fired past the keeper. *3–0!*

Malitoli made the most of another Mali mistake. *4–0!*

That was the same scoreline as their famous victory against Italy back in 1988. What a remarkably resilient team Zambia were! Less than a year after that tragic plane crash, they had bounced back to reach the final of the Africa Cup of Nations. There were big celebrations on the pitch in Tunis and back home in Lusaka too.

Now, if they could just beat Nigeria, Zambia would be crowned the new Champions of Africa. Before kick-off, the two teams were greeted by two very special guests: French legend Michel Platini and the 'King of Football' himself, Pelé.

'Good luck!' the Brazilian said, hugging each and every one of them.

The final began brilliantly for Zambia. They won an

early corner-kick and, in a crowded penalty area, Litana leaped highest. *1–0!*

Maybe luck was on their side this time.

Only two minutes later, however, Nigeria scored an equaliser. Zambia battled on bravely, but their opponents were just a little too strong for them. Early in the second-half, Emmanuel Amuneke scored the winner for Nigeria.

Zambia had come so close to pulling off the greatest comeback in African history! Although the players collected their runners-up medals with heavy hearts, they knew that they had done everything they could to make their country proud during a very difficult time.

But this still isn't the end of the Zambian story! In 2012, nearly 20 years after that awful air disaster, the Copper Bullets made it back to the Africa Cup of Nations final again. This time, they took on the Ivory Coast and after 120 minutes of football, plus 15 penalty kicks, Zambia were victorious at last.

And when they were crowned the new Champions of Africa, the Zambia players were standing only a few hundred metres away from the place where the plane had crashed on that day in 1993. The coach, Hervé Renard, dedicated his side's win to the talented players who lost their lives. It was an enormous achievement for the Zambian team and felt like a fitting end to the incredible journey they had been on.

Pelé's Lucky Shirt

Do you believe in luck? Maybe you have a favourite number, or a favourite colour, or even a favourite old pair of lucky socks? Well, in the 1960s, Edson Arantes do Nascimento had an incredibly lucky football shirt.

'Wait a minute, Edson Arantes who?' some of you might be thinking. Sorry, you probably know him by his more famous nickname ... **Pelé!**

Anyway, back to the 1960s, when Pelé was scoring goal after goal after goal for his club Santos. Pelé had already won two World Cups with Brazil and he was the number one superstar in the world. He seemed unstoppable, but then one day, he suddenly stopped scoring goals.

'What?' said the worried fans.

'How?' said his worried teammates and coaches.

'Why?' said worried Pelé himself.

There had to be a reason! After thinking long and hard, 'A-HA!' Pelé finally worked it out. He had been wearing the same white shirt for ages, with a number 10 on the back. But then after playing a game, he had given his lucky shirt to a Santos fan. Now it was gone, and so were the king of football's magical scoring skills. Surely, the two things had to be connected ...

'We need to find my lucky shirt,' Pelé decided, 'and quickly!'

He was so desperate to get it back that he begged one of his friends to look everywhere for it. After searching all over the city of Santos, his friend finally had some good news to share:

'I found it – I found your lucky shirt!'

Pelé was delighted to have it back and wore it in his next match for Santos. Suddenly his scoring skills were back. In no time, the king of football was his sharpshooting best again and went on to win a third World Cup in 1970. And it was all thanks to that lucky shirt ...

Well, not exactly. Pelé's shirt detective hadn't been able to find his favourite old shirt anywhere and so, instead, he had just given Pelé a different Santos shirt to wear! Pelé was none the wiser and Santos were back on a winning streak.

So, perhaps it's time to throw out those lucky old socks after all ...

CHAPTER FIVE

WHO ARE YA?

The One-Game Wonder

'In *my* day ...' Older fans love going on and on about the 'glory years' of the past, don't they? In some ways, though, football was definitely more fun and unbelievable back then. For one thing, supporters often didn't know anything about their club's new signings, and that made everything more mysterious.

'Who are ya?' they would ask, but what they really meant was, 'Are you any good at football?'

But it wasn't easy for football scouts either. Now, thanks to YouTube and Twitter, anyone can watch the highlights of the 'next big thing' from Azerbaijan to Zambia. But back in the 1990s, it was much harder to find out information about players from other countries and who teams should buy. Sometimes, you just had to take a risk ...

In 1996, lots of English clubs received mysterious phone calls from a man claiming to be the AC Milan striker and World Footballer of the Year, George Weah. He wanted to know if they'd be interested in signing his good friend, **Ali Dia**, a talented forward who had played for Paris Saint-Germain and the Senegal national team.

Suspicious yet? Well, most clubs were. They said no straight away, but not Premier League side Southampton. Their manager Graeme Souness was desperate to bring in new players because the team had so many injury problems. A recommendation from George Weah? Sure, why not! Souness invited Dia to come for a trial.

At the time, Dia was playing for a non-league club called Blyth Spartans, but when a Premier League club came calling, he couldn't say no.

At his first training session, Dia didn't impress his new Southampton teammates at all. 'Where did they get this guy from?' they wondered. 'Is he *really* a professional footballer?'

So the next day, the Saints were very surprised to see Dia sitting there in the dressing room ahead of their home game against Leeds United. Was he just there to watch the game? No, when Souness announced his squad, Dia's name was there on the list of subs!

'Oh well,' Southampton's star player Matt Le Tissier thought to himself, 'let's hope that he doesn't have to play in the match.'

But after 30 minutes, Le Tissier got an injury and had to hobble off the pitch. And who did Souness bring on to replace him? Yes, Southampton's new number 33 – Ali Dia! There were other attackers on the bench but, for some strange reason, the manager turned to the trialist.

So, how did he do? As he sprinted on to make his Premier League debut at the Dell, the score was still 0–0. Could Dia save the day for the Saints? Within minutes, midfielder Eyal Berkovic burst forward on the dribble and passed to Dia on the right side of the penalty area. With three players waiting in the middle for a cross, he decided to go for goal instead. Dia's shot was on target at least, but the Leeds goalkeeper Nigel Martyn made a pretty simple save.

That was the only highlight of Dia's dreadful display. For the next 50 minutes, he raced around the pitch as if he didn't know what position he was supposed to be playing. And whenever he got the ball, his touch was terrible. Le Tissier described him as 'like Bambi on ice'!

The Southampton fans couldn't believe what they were seeing. Dia was hopeless. The club had made bad signings in the past, but never *this* bad.

'HE RAN AROUND THE PITCH LIKE BAMBI ON ICE. IT WAS VERY, VERY EMBARRASSING TO WATCH.'

– Matt Le Tissier

'You don't know what you're doing!' they shouted angrily. 'Get him off!'

Eventually, Souness did sub off his sub in the 85th minute. By then, however, the damage had been done and Leeds had won the game.

Surprise, surprise – that was Dia's one and only Premier League appearance. When the Southampton players turned up for training on Monday morning, there was no sign of their new Senegalese signing. Apparently, he had checked out of his hotel too.

Dia had disappeared, but the fans didn't forget about their one-game wonder. It was all fun at first, but then people started asking serious questions:

1) Where had Dia gone?

A few weeks after his Saints disaster, he signed for non-league club Gateshead. This time, he did score on his debut, but he didn't last long there either.

And 2) More importantly, who was Ali Dia, and did he really know George Weah?

When someone asked the man himself, the real George Weah said that he had never phoned Souness, or even heard of Ali Dia. And the Senegal national team said the same thing:

'Ali *who?*'

It turned out that Dia had played football in France, but for lower league club Saint-Quentin, not Paris Saint-Germain!

When the trick became clear, Dia insisted he hadn't lied. Instead, he just blamed it on someone else:

'I've been made to look a con man, it's not true. I employed an agent when I came to England and he is the con man. He must have been calling all these clubs pretending to be George.'

The mystery of Ali Dia is still one of the funniest and most intriguing stories in the history of English football. The moral of the tale? Never judge someone until you've actually seen them play!

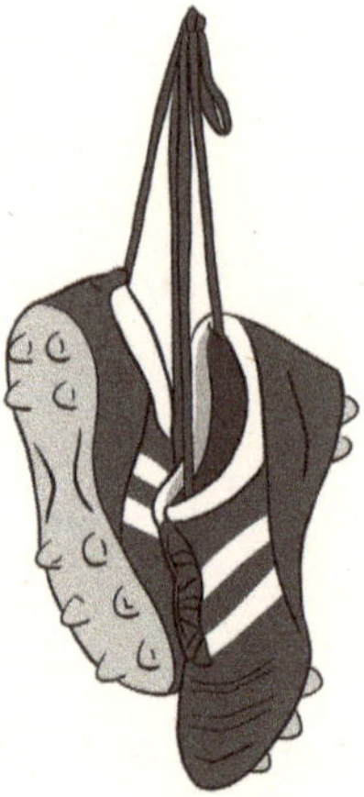

Football's Greatest Conman

Growing up in Brazil in the 1980s, every kid dreamed of becoming a star footballer – 'the next Pelé', 'the next Zico', 'the next Sócrates'. It wasn't just the goals and the trophies that they wanted; it was also the fun, the fame and the lifestyle. But one boy in Rio de Janeiro was absolutely determined to escape poverty and achieve footballing fame, no matter what. His name was Carlos Henrique Raposo, or **Carlos 'Kaiser'** as he soon became known – one of football's greatest conmen!

Carlos got the name 'Kaiser' when he was only ten years old and starring for the Botafogo youth team. Yes, it's important to say at this stage: he was a pretty good young player. With his big hair and confident ball skills, Carlos's teammates even compared him to the Germany captain, Franz Beckenbauer. Beckenbauer's nickname was 'The Kaiser' and so that became Carlos's nickname too.

As he got a bit older, however, Carlos became less interested in the skills and tactics of football, and more interested in its influence and power. If he walked, talked and felt like a footballer, couldn't he just convince the world that he was one too? That way, he would be able to enjoy all the glory off the pitch, without doing any of the hard work on it.

And amazingly, he succeeded. When he was released by Botafogo at the age of 16, Kaiser immediately got a trial at Flamengo, the biggest club in Brazil. How? He knew the son of their youth team coach and tricked his way in. What followed was an incredible 24-year 'career', all without playing a single official football match.

'How on earth did he get away with it?' you're probably wondering by now. Well, Kaiser was very, very cunning. If he hadn't decided to become a 'footballer' instead, he could have been an excellent actor. He could talk his way into – or out of – any situation. There were three key steps in the Kaiser masterplan:

1) Ask famous football friends, like Renato Gaúcho and Carlos Alberto, to recommend him to a new team.

2) Become best friends with whoever is in charge of the club.

And most important of all:

3) Do whatever it takes to avoid playing football for as long as possible.

That last part was the hardest, but Kaiser knew every clever trick in the book.

At Club Puebla in Mexico, he fell to the floor and faked a hamstring injury on the very first day of training. Two years later, he was still there, still claiming that he was getting back to full fitness. Out of all the many excuses he used not to play, injury was easily Kaiser's favourite. It was way before the days of YouTube and Twitter, so he could get away with it again and again.

When he'd had enough of idling around at Independiente in Argentina, he told them that he had to return home for his grandmother's funeral. That lie worked so well that Kaiser used it again on three other occasions!

It was all going well for him at Bangu in Brazil, until the club owner Castor de Andrade became desperate to see his signing play. One night, as he was partying hard, Kaiser got the news that he would be on the bench for their game the next day.

'What?' he cried out in disbelief.

The club manager Moises named him as a substitute. After 15 minutes of the match, Bangu were 2–0 down and Castor called Moises telling him to put Kaiser on up front. Uh oh, was football's greatest trickster finally about to get found out?

For the first time ever, Kaiser was seriously scared.

As he warmed up along the touchline, he was still desperately looking for a way out. Could he pull up with another injury? No, the Bangu fans weren't going to fall for that one again. They already hated him and shouted rude words as he jogged past ...

A-ha! In a flash, Kaiser jumped over a fence and started fighting with his own team's supporters. The referee sent him off before he had even stepped onto the pitch!

'OK, but surely Bangu kicked Kaiser out after that?' you're probably thinking. No, somehow, he managed to talk his way out of that one too. He claimed that the fans had been criticising Castor and he was just sticking up for him. Not only did the club owner believe his friend, but he also gave him a big new contract to say thank you! Unbelievable.

Kaiser, however, decided that it was best not to stick

around, just in case Castor asked him to play again. So, he spoke to his famous friends and managed to get a big move to French team Gazélec Ajaccio. He was happy posing for photos in his new club's kit, but then they asked him to take a few shots at goal before the training session began. Training? 'No thanks!' Kaiser thought to himself. So one by one, he booted all the balls high into the crowd instead.

That was the end of that training session, and those were the only Kaiser kicks that the Ajaccio supporters would ever get to see. European football turned out to be a bit boring and professional for him but, like all good conmen, he always had a Plan B.

Soon, Kaiser was back where he belonged: Brazil. There, his cunning ways continued. On the few occasions when he was forced to train, he hid his lack of skill by staying as far away from the football as possible. That way, his movement looked good, and no one could tell about his poor touch.

There was nothing that Kaiser wouldn't try to keep his footballer dream alive. Sometimes, he pretended to have phone conversations with other clubs in order to get new contracts. Really, he was just talking to himself, and often using a toy phone! Other times, he bribed physios to keep quiet about his fake hamstring injury, and journalists to write made-up articles about his footballing success. One time, he even paid one of the youth players to foul him with a terrible tackle!

Using all of these tricks and more, Kaiser kept his place as the King of Rio de Janeiro throughout the 1980s and 1990s. By then, teams didn't even care about his lack of football talent; they just wanted to have him around for his larger-than-life character. Kaiser was fun and everyone's friend; he was famous for the part he played *off* the pitch.

'I WANTED TO BE AMONG THE OTHER PLAYERS. I JUST DIDN'T WANT TO PLAY.'

In July 2003, aged 40, the world's greatest fake footballer decided to retire. You can't help but admire Kaiser for all that he achieved, although there's no way that you could get away with that in today's game. His career stats speak for themselves: 24 years, 0 games, 0 goals.

The Fake Football Friendly

So far, the stories in this chapter have come from the 1980s and 1990s. But here's a more modern tale for you, about a team apparently playing two games at exactly the same time in completely different places. Unbelievable, right?

In September 2010, the small Middle Eastern island of **Bahrain** was preparing to compete in the West Asian Football Federation Championship. At the time, their national team was ranked 69th in the world, but they had much higher ambitions. So before the tournament began, their coach, Josef Hickersberger, decided to test his players in a friendly match against **Togo**, an African nation who had played at the 2006 World Cup.

As the match kicked off, the Bahrain players were expecting their biggest challenge yet. OK, so Togo's star man, Emmanuel Adebayor, wasn't in the squad, and they didn't recognise any of the names, but 'The Sparrowhawks' would probably have plenty of other talented footballers.

Bahrain thought wrong. By half-time, the Togo team had totally run out of energy. For the rest of the game, their players swung tired legs at the ball, or just stood around watching as the goals went in. What was the reason for their truly terrible performance – the hot day, the long flight from Africa, the absence of Adebayor? Surely it couldn't be any of those things; they were supposed to be professional footballers!

With their opponents giving up, Bahrain cruised to a comfortable 3–0 victory. A win was a win, but Hickersberger couldn't help feeling disappointed: 'They were not fit enough to play 90 minutes; the match was very boring.'

The Bahrain boss was also more than a bit suspicious. They had received a Togo squad list in the build-up to the game, but then just before kick-off, one of the opposition coaches had handed over a completely different list of names. So, was it really the official Togo national team that Bahrain had beaten so easily?

This is where the story gets interesting. When the Togo Football Federation heard about their shock international defeat, they were totally mystified.

'We have not sent any team of footballers to Bahrain,' the federation's president Seyi Memene declared angrily.

The real squad was actually on its way back from an Africa Cup of Nations qualifier against Botswana. There was no way that the Togo national team could be in two places at once.

So in that case, who were those players out on the pitch in the Middle East, wearing the national team shirt and pretending to be Togo? The obvious answer was: they were fakes! But it took their football federation a little longer to find out the full story. It turned out that they were a group of footballers from Togo's first division, who were recruited by a coach called Bana Tchanilé.

Believe it or not, Tchanilé had actually been the manager of the real Togo national team back in 2000. However, ten years later, he had gone from hero to villain, and he received a two-year football ban. Want to guess what he did to get that ban? In July 2010, Tchanilé had taken a fake Togo team to a tournament in Egypt! If at first you don't succeed, try again. So two months later, he had used the same trick in Bahrain.

But why? What was in it for Tchanilé? The coach

insisted that it had nothing to do with money. Instead, it was a protest about the national team not giving young players a chance. He also assured the Togo Football Federation that he had organised the whole thing all on his own. Then things got a little more complicated ... The Bahrain FA had actually set up the friendly match through an agent called Wilson Perumal, who had previously been charged with match-fixing. Perumal denied doing anything wrong, but from a man who admitted fixing football matches, it's hard to know who to believe!

Sadly, at the West Asian Football Federation Championship, Bahrain were knocked out in the group stage. But imagine if they had played the real Togo team that day. Who knows how well they might have done!

The Girl They Called 'Ray'

So far in this chapter, we've had a Premier League flop, football's greatest ever conman and a fake national football team. But sometimes, players have to use disguises for serious reasons, just to be able to play the sport they love.

Growing up as a young girl in London, **Rachel Yankey** was totally football mad. She loved nothing more than kicking a ball around with the boys who lived on her street. At the age of eight, she only thought of football as a fun sport to play in the park; she didn't even know that England had a women's team.

But her friends could see how talented Rachel was and so when they joined a local football club, they invited her to come along too. Why not? When she turned up at her first training session, however, there was a problem: it was a boys' football team, and she was a girl.

Rachel was still desperate to join and the coach, Tony Chelsea, didn't want to stop her from playing, especially once he had seen how skilful she was. So in the end, the team came up with a clever plan:

1) They took Rachel to a barber shop and got her hair cut short (her mum was not at all happy about that!),

and

2) They decided to call her 'Ray' instead.

Why Ray? Well, that's what you get when you spell out the initials of her full name:

RACHEL

ABA

YANKEY

For the next two years, 'Ray' was the star of her local team. But the older she got, and the better she played, the harder it became to keep her secret. Eventually, the truth came out, and with Tony Chelsea's help, Yankey moved to a girls-only team called Mill Hill United.

That was the end of 'Ray', but only the start of Rachel Yankey, The Footballer. Now that she had found a place where she could be herself, there was no stopping her as she flew down the left wing.

In 1996, aged 16, Yankey signed for Arsenal and won the FA Women's National Premier League title in her first season.

A year later, she scored on her England debut.

And aged 20, Yankey became the first-ever professional female player in England, leading the way for the next generation of Lionesses. As Lucy Bronze said recently, 'I remember watching Kelly Smith and

Rachel Yankey play for England on TV and I wanted to be like them.'

By 2007, Yankey was the most famous female footballer in England. She was chosen to model the new national team kit alongside male stars like Steven Gerrard and Michael Owen. Yankey went on to play 129 matches for her country, scoring 19 goals including one at the 2011 Women's World Cup. She also won a whopping 28 trophies with clubs including Arsenal, Fulham and the New Jersey Wildcats in the USA.

But Yankey's greatest achievement may well be the way that she changed the image of women's football forever. The silky skills, the friendly smile, the fun coaching videos – who wouldn't want to be like Rachel Yankey when they're older? And look what she started: 20 years later, football-mad girls now grow up pretending to be Ellen White or Alex Morgan, rather than 'Ray'.

A Faked Death and a Game of Football

If you're lucky enough to become a football superstar, you've got to make the most of that moment. That's certainly what Denmark's pocket-sized striker, **Allan Simonsen**, was thinking in 1977.

That year, he led his German club Borussia Mönchengladbach to the Bundesliga title and the European Cup final, plus he won the European Player of the Year award too. But before all that, Simonsen had a different kind of starring role to play.

On 1 May, the Denmark national team took on Poland in a crucial World Cup qualifier. The two nations were competing with Portugal for just one spot at the 1978 tournament in Argentina. If Denmark lost, their World Cup dream would be over. So, the country was counting on their number 9 to shine.

Simonsen certainly did that. After Poland scored an early goal, Denmark pushed forward on the attack, looking for their little striker. As a cross came towards him, Simonsen leaped up high to head the ball goalwards, but the keeper tipped it over the crossbar. *Corner-kick!*

As his teammate ran over to take it, Simonsen waited in the box, bouncing on his toes. He was ready for his big moment. The cross was coming straight towards him and Simonsen sprang up into the air, but at the last second, he fell to the floor and missed the ball completely.

Oh no, what had happened? It was as if he'd been shot in the back by a rooftop sniper. Well, that wasn't too far away from the truth.

At the time, a Danish director called Tom Hedegaard was making an action film called *The Marksman*. The plot of the movie: a famous footballer is murdered during a major match. But Hedegaard didn't have enough money to shoot the scene properly, so he asked Simonsen to perform the role in real life instead!

For some reason, the Danish striker agreed and, to his credit, he put a lot of effort into his acting performance. After collapsing near the penalty spot, Simonsen lay there, totally still, for several seconds as his worried teammates surrounded him. Was he hurt? Was he *dead*? No, all of a sudden, he came back to life and carried on playing.

With his acting role completed, Simonsen returned to what he did best: scoring goals. Early in the second-half, he burst forward and fired a left-foot shot into the bottom corner. *1–1!* The Danish striker punched the air with both fists like a true action hero. He had saved the day after all.

Unfortunately, Poland then scored again five minutes later, and the match finished 2–1. Denmark were defeated and now they definitely wouldn't be playing at the 1978 World Cup. As they left the stadium, their sad supporters must have been wondering, ‘What if Simonsen had scored from that corner in the first-half? What was that dramatic dive all about?’

They soon found out, when they went to see The Marksman in the cinema. Football star or movie star? As the strange story of Allan Simonsen shows, it’s not easy to be both.

CHAPTER SIX

FOR THE LOVE OF THE GAME

Saving Lives on the Pitch

Not all superheroes wear capes; some wear football kits.

Until 30 March 2014, **Jaba Kankava** just seemed like your average footballer. He was a tough-tackling midfielder for his country, Georgia, and for FC Dnipro, one of the top teams in the Ukrainian Premier League.

That fateful day, Kankava's club were playing at home, taking on their big rivals, Dynamo Kyiv, in one of the most important matches of the season. If Dnipro lost, Shakhtar Donetsk would almost certainly win the league title instead.

'Come on you Warriors of the Light!' the home fans cheered loudly. (Cool nickname, right?)

In the 20th minute, the Dnipro goalkeeper Denys

Boyko came off his line to make an easy catch. But as he jumped up for the ball, his knee accidentally struck the Kyiv captain Oleh Husyev in the head.

The game carried on, but fortunately Kankava had noticed that something was seriously wrong. Husyev was lying there, sprawled across the grass and he wasn't moving. He had been knocked unconscious by Boyko's knee.

Yes, Dnipro were desperate to win, but this was far more important than a football match. It was a matter of life and death, and their courageous Georgian midfielder had to do something to help.

Kankava to the rescue! The midfielder rushed straight over and rolled Husyev onto his back. Right, what next? The Dnipro man was in doctor mode; he would have to act fast to save Husyev's life. He could tell that his opponent wasn't breathing, and his teeth were clamped shut. So

Kankava had to use all his strength to open Husyev's jaws, and then stick his fingers down the player's throat to stop him swallowing his tongue.

The atmosphere in the Dnipro stadium grew quiet and sombre. 'Is he going to be OK?' both sets of supporters wondered. In that moment, their football rivalry stopped and both sides came together. Everyone just held their breath and hoped for the best for Husyev.

Down on the pitch, the Kyiv players were screaming and shouting in panic, but Kankava stayed calm and focused. Eventually, Husyev bit down hard on his fingers. 'Arggghhh!' Kankava cried out in agony, but at least it meant that the Kyiv captain was conscious again. With the help of teammates and real doctors, Kankava finally managed to free his opponent's tongue and clear his airway. Husyev lay there coughing and confused but hey, he was alive and breathing! That was the main thing.

The club doctors helped Husyev to his feet and then carried him off on a stretcher, with applause ringing out around the stadium. When they got to the hospital, there was good news; the Kyiv captain had a mild concussion and a bruised jaw, but amazingly, there were no other injuries. It was a miracle and Husyev had his opponent Kankava to thank for that. 'He saved Oleh's life,' one of the doctors confirmed.

As the match kicked off again, the Dnipro midfielder was the hero of the hour. Kankava's super-quick reaction had helped keep Husyev alive. The Dynamo Kyiv players hugged and thanked him, while their fans clapped and cheered. At Kyiv's next match, they held up a brand-new banner:

'KANKAVA – RESPECT'

Although football suddenly didn't seem so important, Dnipro did go on to beat Dynamo Kyiv 2–0. However, it was their rivals Shakhtar who lifted the Ukrainian Premier League title.

And what about Kankava? Well, he had a big bite mark to show for his heroics, and soon his inspiring story had spread all over the world. He was now famous for more than just his football skills. A few weeks later, the Ukrainian government even awarded him a special medal for bravery.

Kankava now plays for FC Tobol in Kazakhstan. The Georgian hasn't saved any more lives yet, but his teammates and opponents must feel a whole lot safer knowing that they have a real-life superhero with them on the pitch.

The Trailblazer Behind the Women's World Cup

Lucy Bronze, Megan Rapinoe, Sam Kerr ... at France 2019, the top female footballers showed off their skills in front of millions of spectators from all over the globe. In the UK, more people watched the semi-final between England and the USA than they did the 2019 men's Champions League final between Liverpool and Tottenham. But it wasn't always that way. Once upon a time, less than 30 years ago, there was no such thing as a Women's World Cup. And if it wasn't for some brave trailblazers, who knows, women's football might never have had a major international tournament of its own.

The 1970s was an exciting new era for women's football. In England, for example, the sport was no longer banned, and the FA launched a new club tournament called 'The Mitre Trophy', which later became the Women's FA Cup. In 1972, England selected their first-ever official women's national team and in their first match, they beat Scotland, just like the Lionesses did 47 years later at the 2019 World Cup.

There were similar signs of progress in other countries as well. In 1970, women were finally allowed to play football in China. That same year, the first unofficial Women's World Cup took place, with Denmark beating Italy in the final. Twelve months later, Denmark's 15-year-old forward Susanne Augustesen scored a hat-trick to defeat Mexico in front of over 100,000 supporters. In 1973, Sweden launched their first national team, followed by Norway, Thailand, Australia and many others. And from 1979, females in Brazil could show off their samba skills too.

At last, women's football was taking over the world! The next step seemed clear: an official Women's World Cup. After all, the men's tournament had been going strong since 1930. It was about time that women were allowed to shine too. But when the female footballers asked for their own competition, FIFA said no. The men weren't ready to share the limelight yet.

That all changed in 1986, thanks to an amazing woman called **Ellen Wille**. Back home in Norway, Wille is known as the mother of women's football. In 1976, she was so fed up with the sexism in the Norwegian Football Federation (NFF) that she became their first female member. With her help, the sport had grown bigger and bigger: more pitches, more referees, more coaches and, best of all, more fantastic footballers.

After ten years of fighting hard to promote women's football in her own country, Wille decided to focus on an even greater goal: growing the game internationally. In order to do that, she needed to talk to the most important people in world football. So she travelled to FIFA's 45th Congress meeting in Mexico City to make the biggest speech of her life. She was doing it on behalf of the NFF, but also on behalf of women's football all over the globe.

She had every reason to feel nervous as she stepped up to the microphone; she was about to make history as the first female to speak in front of FIFA. But when her moment arrived, Wille stood up bravely in front of the 150 men in the room and made her message clear:

'It's time for change!'

Wille pointed out that women's football was hardly mentioned in any of the FIFA documents. 'Why not?' she demanded to know. 'It's the same game, isn't it? With the same-sized ball, the same number of players, and the same 90-minute matches?'

The men in the room couldn't disagree with that. Wille simply wanted equal opportunities for female footballers. Women, she argued, deserved the chance to play at the Olympic Games and, most of all, they deserved to have their own World Cup.

At last, Wille's words forced the FIFA men to listen. The story goes that the President João Havelange turned to the General Secretary Sepp Blatter and said, 'From now, you must remember the women's football!' They liked the idea of a Women's World Cup, but first, they wanted to test it out. How high was the quality of football, and how many people would come to watch women play?

So, two years later, they organised the 1988 FIFA Women's Invitation Tournament, or International Women's Football Tournament. It took place in China and 12 nations were invited to compete:

From Australia came ... Australia.

From Asia: China, Japan and Thailand.

From Africa: Ivory Coast.

From North America: Canada and the USA.

From South America: Brazil.

And from Europe: Netherlands, Norway, Sweden and Czechoslovakia (it's divided into 'Czech Republic' and 'Slovakia' these days).

In the final, Wille's Norway beat Sweden 1–0 in front of over 30,000 supporters. It turned out that women's football was awesome and plenty of people enjoyed watching it! The tournament was declared a huge success and so, in 1991, they did it all over again. This time, however, it was officially known as the 'FIFA Women's World Cup'. Progress, at last!

Sadly for Wille, Norway lost to the USA in the final, but she was delighted to see the results of her brave actions.

'Women's football has taken a huge step forward. Women are playing the game all over the world now.'

Since 1991, the Women's World Cup has grown more and more popular, just as Wille hoped and dreamed. Over 750 million people around the world watched the 2015 tournament on TV, and that number was even higher for 2019.

There's still more work to be done, though. Modern

female football heroes such as Ada Hegerberg and Marta continue to fight for equal pay and equal respect. It makes you wonder: if it wasn't for Wille's inspiring speech, how long would it have been before women's football was taken seriously?

The Injured Keeper Who Became an FA Cup Hero

Most players will suffer injuries at some point in their career, no matter how small. There are always medics on hand to help when this happens. But sometimes players will carry on playing, even when they really shouldn't! One such player was **Bert Trautmann**. In the 1956 FA Cup final, underdogs Manchester City were winning 3–1 with less than 20 minutes to go. Their victory wasn't certain yet, however. The Birmingham City attack kept threatening their goal, and they might well have scored again if it wasn't for Manchester City's sweeper-keeper, Bert Trautmann.

The German had just won the Footballer of the Year award and he was showing everyone why. Having set up

Manchester City's third goal with a long throw, he was now keeping his team in the game.

First, he rushed out bravely to beat Birmingham striker Eddy Brown to the through-ball.

'Nice one, Trautmann!' the fans cheered.

Then, he dived down to catch a cross just as Peter Murphy was about to pounce.

'We love you, Bert!'

But this time, Trautmann didn't jump back up to his feet like he usually did. Instead, he lay there, barely moving in his six-yard box.

'What's wrong?' his worried teammates asked, standing over him.

He had really hurt himself in that heroic challenge with Murphy. Eventually, the Manchester City players managed to help him up, but it was clear that Trautmann was in excruciating pain. As he staggered back to his goal-line, he cried out in agony, clutching the back of his neck.

'Bert, there's no way you can continue – it could be serious,' the team physio, Laurie Barnett, argued sensibly.

In those days, however, there was no such thing as substitutes. If he went off, Manchester City would be down to ten men and one of their outfield players would have to go in goal.

'Don't worry, Roy Little will take your place,' the captain Roy Paul tried to convince his keeper.

'No, I'm fine,' Trautmann told him, battling on bravely. His team needed him and maybe he could get away with not doing very much in the last 14 minutes ...

No chance! The Manchester City defenders did their best to protect their injured keeper, but Birmingham still believed that they could win the FA Cup final. They pushed forward at every opportunity.

A Birmingham midfielder chipped the ball over Dave Ewing's head to Brown, who chested it down and pulled his leg back to shoot ...

SAVED! Playing through the pain, Trautmann threw himself down at the striker's feet.

Murphy raced down the right wing, towards the Manchester City goal ...

SAVED! Trautmann charged out again and cleared the danger.

Although the Manchester City keeper was suffering badly, he refused to give up. The year before, they had made it all the way to Wembley, but lost to Newcastle United in the final. This time, they were so close to glory. Like the fans in the stands, Trautmann counted down the last minutes: *5, 4, 3, 2, 1 ... FINAL WHISTLE!*

Manchester City were the FA Cup winners and Trautmann was the man of the match. When he left the field in a daze of agony and ecstasy, the crowd cheered loudly for their hero:

For he's a jolly good fellow ...

As he climbed the Wembley steps with his teammates to collect the trophy, Trautmann could feel the pain in his neck getting worse. But he wouldn't miss this amazing moment for the world.

'Are you sure you're all right?' the Duke of Edinburgh questioned as he shook his hand and gave him his winners' medal.

'Yes, thanks,' the keeper replied, with his neck at a crooked angle.

By the time he arrived at Manchester City's winners' banquet that evening, Trautmann couldn't move his head at all. He hoped that it might heal by the morning, but no, when he woke up, the pain was still just as bad as before. So he went to see a doctor, who told him that it was just a crick in his neck, and nothing to worry about.

'Thanks, what a relief!' Trautmann said when he heard the good news.

A couple of days later, however, it was still hurting, and so he decided to get a second opinion. This time, the doctor took an X-ray and came to a very different conclusion: Trautmann had broken his neck badly.

'You're lucky to still be alive!' the doctor declared.

Seven months later, Trautmann was back in action, saving the day for City again, and he played on for another eight seasons at the club.

But winning the FA Cup with a broken neck was just one of the many challenges that Trautmann had to face during his remarkable life.

When the Second World War began, he was an athletic 16-year-old who was training to be a car mechanic in his homeland, Germany. But a few years later, Trautmann found himself fighting in Adolf Hitler's army, against the English, and winning five medals for his bravery. But in 1945, he was captured and later taken to a prisoner-of-war camp in Lancashire. There, aged 23, he changed his name from 'Bernd' to 'Bert' and his position from striker to goalkeeper.

Soon after the end of the war, Trautmann was offered the chance to return to Germany but, instead, he decided to stay in England and work his way up through the football leagues. That was far from easy, though, because of his past. During those post-war years, England could be a very difficult place for foreigners, and especially Germans. Wherever Trautmann played, people called him 'Nazi' or 'war criminal', or even worse names. All he could do was ignore it, just like his neck pain that day at Wembley.

Driven by anger and guilt for what he had seen

and done during the Second World War, Trautmann soon became a star keeper at St Helens Town. When he then signed for Manchester City in 1949, their fans were furious. How could they even think about having a former German soldier in their squad? Some threatened to boycott the club, while others sent nasty, angry letters directly to Trautmann.

He didn't let that stop him, though, and seven years later, he was an FA Cup winner and fans were calling him by more affectionate names like 'Old Bert'. The German keeper had become a Manchester City and an English hero.

'I WAS BORN A GERMAN, BUT IN MY HEART I'M BRITISH. I HAD SO MUCH KINDNESS, FRIENDLINESS, AND UNDERSTANDING SHOWN TO ME. SO I STAYED. AND I'M GLAD I STAYED.'

The Flying Football Stars

When you think of football, you might think of Premier League superstars playing in gigantic stadiums. But really, football is a game that anyone can play anywhere; all you need is a ball and something to use as goalposts. Easy! The simple joys of football can help bring normal people together through the toughest of times. Nothing proves that better than the sensational **Salone Flying Stars**.

Between 1991 and 2002, there was a terrible, violent war in the west African nation of Sierra Leone. Eventually, the fighting stopped, but a lot of survivors were left with very serious injuries. Some had lost arms; many had lost legs. And the problems also ran much deeper than that. Now that the war was over, many amputees felt lonely and helpless. What were they supposed to do with the rest of their lives? In Sierra Leone, there were so many people who were desperate for food and jobs, but it was especially hard for disabled people. They struggled to find work, attend school or live a normal life. It was so sad and unfair. There had to be something they could do to fight for change in their country.

One day, an American nurse called Dee Malchow visited a camp in Sierra Leone's capital city, Freetown. When she spoke to the local people, she soon discovered their passion for football.

'Don't give up – you can still play the game!' Malchow encouraged them. She was an amputee herself, and she knew that playing sport could bring so much happiness during difficult times. It can be the best way to build your confidence back up.

'Really?' the locals asked her eagerly. 'How?'

As soon as she returned to the USA, Malchow sent a special parcel to Sierra Leone. Inside were the rules of amputee football, a video of the game, and a box of sport shoes. That was everything they needed to kick things off.

So, in 2003, a new football club was formed, called Salone Flying Stars. There, the local amputees could make new friends and share stories, all while playing the sport they loved. Football gave these men and women a new community to feel part of, and a new pride and positivity.

'I PRAY THAT, THROUGH SALONE FLYING STARS, I CAN IMPROVE MY LIFE.'

– **Mohamed Jalloh**

'It moves our mind and gives us hope,' says Mohamed Jalloh, one of the longest-serving Flying Stars. 'Whenever people stand and watch us, we think it's very important to the nation.'

It did, however, take the players a while to get used to the new form of football. It required a lot of strength and very good balance. At first, when people saw them practising, they laughed and made cruel jokes, but the Flying Stars didn't listen. They were determined to prove those people wrong by mastering their sport. Soon, they were flying down the sandy pitch thanks to the crutches that the club gave them, showing off their football skills. The game is really exhausting for the arms and the leg, but it's also loads of fun. The rules are really simple:

1) No touching the ball with your crutches.

2) No touching the ball with your injured leg.

Other than that, you can do anything you like: weaving dribbles, sliding tackles, swerving shots and, of course, cool celebrations.

The goalkeeper is the only player with two legs, but they are still amputee players and usually only have one arm. That doesn't stop them making super saves, though.

And Salone Flying Stars aren't the only amputee football club in Sierra Leone; there's also the Single Leg Amputee Sports Association and the Flying Eagles. Sunday is football day in Freetown, and that's when these teams meet up to play against each other every week. These days, local people often go down to the beach to watch their fast, ferocious battles.

But the Salone Flying Stars are about much more than just football. Although the game gives the players friendship and fun, they still need jobs, homes, food and money in order to support themselves and their families. Together, they're fighting for a brighter future for disabled people in Sierra Leone. Their demands to the government are as simple as the rules of the game they love:

1) More rights.

2) More opportunities to work and study.

Football has helped show the Flying Stars that there is so much that they can achieve in their lives, just as long as they get the chance.

An Awkward Minute's Silence

It's always nice to see football clubs taking a real interest in the lives of their most loyal fans. However, it is very important to check the facts first.

Congleton Town, a football club from north-west England, learned that lesson the hard way. In March 1993, Chris Phillips was about to hand out the programmes for Congleton's match against Rossendale when the club secretary gave him some very sad news. Fred Cope, Congleton's oldest supporter, had died at the age of 85.

In that emotional moment, Phillips burst into action. He quickly wrote a short but touching tribute to Fred and stapled copies to all the programmes. He also informed the referee that they would need a minute's silence before kick-off. The one thing Phillips hadn't done, however, was confirm the sad news with anyone. He just took the secretary's word for it.

There was a melancholy atmosphere around Congleton Town Football Club that day, as their supporters gathered to say goodbye to an old friend. But just as the players walked out onto the pitch at the Booth Street stadium, the 'dead man' appeared. Was it a ghost? No, it turned out that Fred had been ill, but not that ill. In fact, he wasn't even ill enough to miss a match!

When Phillips spotted the club's oldest fan still standing, his heart skipped a beat. He was pleased to see Fred, of course, but it was all a little awkward. He wasn't supposed to be alive! Oh well, it was too late to change anything now. The two teams were already lining up around the centre-circle to pay their respects.

'There will now be a minute's silence in honour of ... Bobby Moore,' Phillips announced, showing off some very quick thinking. England's World Cup-winning captain had died only a few days earlier, so it didn't seem strange at all.

Phew, had they got away with their mistake? Not really, because someone soon showed Fred a copy of the matchday programme. Oh dear, was that the end of Fred Cope, the Congleton Town fan? No, fortunately he saw the funny side of the misunderstanding. His team won 6–1 and Fred even won a prize in the half-time raffle. Not a bad day for a man that everyone thought was dead!

CONCLUSION

So, now that you've finished reading *Unbelievable Football*, do you love the beautiful game more than ever? I hope so! And after you've argued with your mates over your favourite facts and stories, I hope that you'll feel inspired to get out on the pitch or playground and create some unbelievable football moments of your own.

Well, what are you waiting for? Grab your ball and go!

ACKNOWLEDGEMENTS

Like the best football clubs, this book has been a true team effort. First and foremost, I'd like to thank the manager, my editor Laura Horsley, the brains behind *Unbelievable Football*. Without her coaching and clever tactical plans, this book would have finished bottom of the league! And I'd also like to thank the Director of Football, my agent, Nick Walters, the dealmaker and a man who knows how to keep his players happy.

And last but by no means least, where would a football club be without its fans? So thanks and love go to all my friends and family for their loyal support. Especially Iona, who encouraged me to take on this exciting new challenge in the first place, and then cheered me on every step of the way.

REFERENCES

The Elephants Who Played for Peace

Hayes, Alex. 'Didier Drogba brings peace to the Ivory Coast.' Telegraph.co.uk. 08 August 2007. www.telegraph.co.uk/sport/football/international/2318500/Didier-Drogba-brings-peace-to-the-Ivory-Coast.html, accessed 02 July 2019.

The Lancashire Lasses Who Changed Football

Newsham, Gail J. *In A League Of Their Own: The Dick, Kerr Ladies 1917–1965.* London: Paragon Publishing, 2014.

The Superstar Manager Who Survived the War

Gonçalves, Pedro. 'The greatest teams of all time: Benfica 1960–62.' UEFA.com. 15 June 2015. www.uefa.com/uefachampionsleague/news/newsid=2253538.html, accessed 23 June 2019.

The Shepherd Boy Who Stopped Ronaldo

Jafarzadeh, Behnam. 'Alireza Beiranvand: from sleeping rough to the World Cup with Iran.' TheGuardian.com. 01 June 2018. www.theguardian.com/football/2018/jun/01/alireza-beiranvand-sleeping-rough-world-cup-iran-goalkeeper, accessed 16 June 2019.

Leicester City, the Unbelievable Season

'Ranieri tells fans "keep dreaming, why wake up".' BBC.co.uk. 07 May 2016. www.bbc.co.uk/sport/av/football/36239491, accessed 20 June 2019.

The Remarkable Rise of Queen Fara

Watts, Matt. 'How Fara Williams went from homeless to England's most capped footballer.' Independent.co.uk. 12 January 2017. www.independent.co.uk/news/homelesshelpline/fara-williams-englands-most-capped-footballer-from-home-less-to-womens-football-international-a7524401.html, accessed 24 June 2019.

The World Cup Star Who Saved His Best Until Last

Magambo, Placide. 'An Exclusive Interview With Africa's Favorite Footballer, Roger Milla.' Okayafrica.com. 07 November 2016. www.okayafrica.com/africas-favorite-footballer-roger-milla-on-his-wild-career-and-his-second-life-as-an-environmentalist/, accessed 02 July 2019.

The Police Dog that Rescued a Team from Relegation

Duzyj, Mickey. 'Losers, Season 1 Episode 2: The Jaws of Victory.' NETFLIX. 01 March 2019.

Paul the Octopus

Collins, Nick. 'Paul the psychic octopus correctly predicts Germany defeat.' Telegraph.co.uk. 08 July 2010. www.telegraph.co.uk/sport/football/world-cup/7878270/Paul-the-psychic-octopus-correctly-predicts-Germany-defeat.html, accessed 12 June 2019.

The Busby Babes

Mehra, Arjun. 'The inspiring story of Sir Matt Busby's leadership and the rise of Manchester United.' Yourstory.com. 29 May 2014. yourstory.com/2014/05/sir-matt-busby, accessed 10 July 2019.

The Miracle of Istanbul

'Before the game ... what they said: ... and the world's post-match verdicts as well as five great games from this season's Champions League.' Guardian.com. 29 May 2005. https://www.theguardian.com/football/2005/may/29/newsstory.sport6, accessed 30 June 2019.

The One-Game Wonder

Smith, Alan. '"What's this geezer doing? He's hopeless" – the Ali Dia story, 20 years on.' Guardian.com. 22 November 2016. www.theguardian.com/football/2016/nov/22/ali-dia-story-20-years-on-southampton-souness, accessed 2019.

Football's Greatest Conman

Smyth, Rob. *Kaiser: The Greatest Footballer Never To Play Football.* London: Yellow Jersey Press, 26 July 2018.

The Injured Keeper Who Became an FA Cup Hero

Clay, Catrine. *Trautmann's Journey: From Hitler Youth to FA Cup Legend.* London: Yellow Jersey Press, 03 March 2011.

The Flying Football Stars

Rice-Coates, Callum. 'Salone Flying Stars: The football club giving a chance to amputees in Sierra Leone.' inews.co.uk. 09 October 2018. inews.co.uk/sport/football/salone-flying-stars-the-football-club-giving-a-chance-to-amputees-in-sierra-leone/, accessed 29 June 2019.